SHORT CUTS

INTRODUCTIONS TO FILM STUDIES

ROMANTIC COMEDY

BOY MEETS GIRL MEETS GENRE

TAMAR JEFFERS MCDONALD

WALLFLOWER

LONDON and NEW YORK

A Wallflower Paperback

First published in Great Britain in 2007 by
Wallflower Press
6a Middleton Place, Langham Street, London, W1W 7TE
www.wallflowerpress.co.uk

A catalogue record for this book is available from the British Library

ISBN 978-1-905674-02-2

Book Design by Rob Bowden Design

Printed in Great Britain by Antony Rowe Ltd, Chippenham, Wiltshire

CONTENTS

ACKNOWLEDGEMENTS

I would like to thank Iris Luppa, John Mercer and Martin Patrick, former colleagues at Buckinghamshire Chilterns University College, for their support and encouragement of this project. Many thanks also to Alisia Chase, Isobel Lane, Robin Larsen, Tom Mulak and Martha Nochimson for kindly shared romcom insights, and to Richard Dyer, whose appreciation of the mixedness of film pleasures continues to inspire me. At Wallflower Press, the keen eye and discerning mind of Jacqueline Downs made this a better book than it would have been without her interventions; Yoram Allon's patience and support were also invaluable.

Special thanks to Chloe and Jessica for watching so many romantic comedies with me without rebellion, and, as always, to Paul for support and love.

INTRODUCTION

There is a moment in *Sleepless in Seattle*, Nora Ephron's 1993 romantic comedy, where one character, Suzy (Rita Wilson), relates to her husband Greg (Victor Garber) her feelings about the romantic 'old movie', *An Affair to Remember* (1957). Recounting the plot, which involves star-crossed lovers meeting, falling in love and nearly failing to reconnect, Suzy begins to cry. Even talking about the film provokes an emotional response. Her male audience is unimpressed, however. 'That's a *chick's* movie!' dismisses Sam (Tom Hanks), mockingly volunteering that *The Dirty Dozen* (1967) is equally moving to male audience members.

I cite this scene here at the start of an investigation of Hollywood romantic comedies because it introduces a trio of important concepts which will recur throughout the book: notions around audiences, self-referentiality and intertextuality, and emotion.

In invoking the older romance, *Sleepless in Seattle* wryly acknowledges both its own fictional status, and its place within a tradition of films about fate and love (the later movie's own couple, Sam and Annie (Meg Ryan), seem doomed to separation just like the earlier duo, but both pairs finally end up together). Suzy's championing of the film and her male companions' dismissal of it testify to the assumption that romantic comedies are films made for and enjoyed by women audience members; to back up this essentialist gender point, Sam's young son (Ross Malinger) also does not 'get' the film, while his friend Jessica (Gaby Hoffman) instantly pronounces it 'the best movie I ever saw!'. Furthermore, the male derision is principally directed at the pleasure Suzy gets from crying over the film: just recounting the story is enough to affect her emotionally. This appeal to tears, an excess of feeling which is permitted release in weeping, is a quality *Sleepless in Seattle* recognises in the 'old movie' it quotes and which it also aims to provoke within its own audience. The men mock this when they pretend to cry recounting the details of Robert Aldrich's tough war film ('Jim Brown throwing the grenades!'; 'Richard Jaeckel and Lee Marvin on top of a tank dressed like Nazis!'). The implication is that women enjoy crying over love stories, even successful ones, whereas men much more calmly watch scenes of destruction where important actions are performed.

Providing another level of meaning within the scene is the fact that the actor playing Suzy, Rita Wilson, is performing arguing with her real-life husband, Tom Hanks, playing Sam. The idea of happy successful heterosexual love is thus in the background even as the characters ostensibly dispute the importance of portrayals of heterosexual love.

In this book we will consider and question the romantic comedy's habitual association with female audience members, recognise and interrogate the genre's inclination towards self-reflexivity and quotation, and discuss the seemingly paradoxical importance of tears to this form of comedy.

Another important idea we can take from the *Sleepless in Seattle* scene is a kind of institutionalised devaluing of the genre. David Shumway, in an insightful book which discusses the tensions between romance and marriage, tellingly notes the habitual neglect such texts receive:

> The love story is so familiar in our culture that we rarely give it a second thought ... 'Boy gets girl, boy loses girl, boy gets girl back' is exhibit A of standard plots in all fictional media. (2003: 157)

Shumway's comment indicates a basic problem with the Hollywood romantic comedy: it employs so formulaic a storyline, is so over-familiar a product, that it is easy to take for granted. What this book seeks to do is turn a spotlight on this area, and ask questions about what elements go into the romantic comedy and why it seems such an obvious film form to overlook or underappreciate.

It should be noted at the outset that, while the romantic comedy is a genre popular with audiences and reproduced within national cinemas around the world, this book takes as its central topic the romantic comedy as made in 'Hollywood', exploring the conventions of romantic comedy as they were established and then modulated over time within mainstream American cinema. This is not to suggest the North American model is the only one: indeed, the different inflections given to the genre by different national contexts are very interesting and provoke revealing comparisons. For example, one of the current elements of the Hollywood 'romcom', as such films are frequently termed,[1] seems to be a de-emphasising of the importance of sex. By contrast, the contemporary British romantic comedy seems comfortable with including pre-marital sex but, fascinatingly, often seeks to excuse this within its narratives by making the sexually aggressive partner both female *and* American, as in *Four Weddings and a Funeral* (1994), *Notting Hill* (1999) and *Wimbledon* (2004).

A recurrent trend in the writing about romantic comedy is to divide it into sub-genres, like the screwball and sex comedies (Babington & Evans 1989: 180; cf Henderson 1978: 12). Writers also tend to assert that these different forms flourished in specific periods: for example, Ted Sennett (1973), Duane Byrge and Robert Milton Miller (1991) and Diane Carson (1994) note screwball lasting from 1934 to around 1942. This book, while examining the usual periodisation, suggests that the specific qualities which inform these sub-genres may be more fluid, providing continuities as well as contrasts, and persisting in the dominant mode of romantic comedy today. Thus, while the chapters here take as their specific topics particular sub-genres and their contextual timeframes, the film examples point to the continuation of certain motifs in the genre. In the screwball chapter, for example, discussion of recent films will augment that of movies from the 1930s, to illustrate the persistent nature of some of its chief characteristics.

Chapter one offers a brief overview of the Hollywood romantic comedy as a whole, discussing how to interrogate a film via its genre, and suggesting why the romantic comedy might traditionally be overlooked. It explores the elements requiring examination in a genre study, and offers a master definition of romantic comedy. Finally, the chapter uses the early work by Colin McArthur (1972) on the iconography of the gangster film, exploring his iconographical categories and applying them to the visual systems employed in the romantic comedy.

Subsequent chapters focus on exploring the characteristics of the screwball comedy, the sex comedy and the most self-consciously radical texts, those from the 1970s. The final chapter traces the continuities and contrasts that current romantic comedies maintain with the earlier forms; in generally returning to a much more conservative ending than the romantic comedies of the 1970s, the contemporary romcom reveals new insecurities and preoccupations underlying its version of the standard boy-meets-girl narrative.

Each of these chapters mentions many key movies, but also presents a detailed analysis of just one exemplary film; the synopses of these are found in Appendix A. In providing these case studies my aim has sometimes been to forgo what might be the canonical, obvious choice (as with perhaps *Bringing Up Baby* (1938), one of the most written-about screwball comedies), in favour of lesser-known movies which exhibit the classic characteristics but also permit fresh analysis. Thus *My Man Godfrey* (1936) and *Pillow Talk* (1959) are closely read to reveal aspects of the screwball and sex comedy respectively. *Annie Hall* (1977), on the other hand, while often discussed, does seem to be the most truly radical of all the 1970s romantic comedies, and thus merits another close look in seeing how it abandons attributes usually treated as indispensable by films of the genre, such as the happy ending. Finally, an analysis of *You've Got Mail* (1998) demonstrates how the current evolution of the romantic comedy has largely chosen to ignore the advances made by the genre in the 1970s, self-consciously reverting instead to more traditional textual strategies.

While I have emphasised that the following chapters will be alert to originating contexts, it should not be believed that films straightforwardly reflect the attitudes of their particular times. As socially created objects, they embody competing impulses, as Frank Krutnik aptly summarises:

> In general one can see generic forms as a functional interface between the cinematic institution, audiences and the wider realm of culture. Films never spring magically from their cultural context, but they represent instead much more complex activities of nego-tiation, addressing cultural transformations in a highly compro-mised and displayed manner ... In the case of romantic comedy, it is particularly important to stress how specific films or cycles mediate between a body of conventionalised 'generic rules' ... and a shifting environment of sexual-cultural codifications. (1990: 57–8).

Thus, while this book sometimes follows the usual writing on romantic comedies by comparing different types of films and their specific chronological contexts, it also intends to problematise the strict relationship of originating moment and film form by showing both the continuation of elements across different historical periods and the contested nature of those elements within the films at the time of their emergence. I hope in this way to prompt some new directions on these films, by analysing and tracing the maintenance or mutation of core elements within them across time. The book will:

- provide definitions of the genre and its sub-genres
- discuss the relation of different sub-genres to their historical contexts
- analyse the dominant characteristics of each sub-genre
- offer closely-read case studies of each sub-genre
- examine the ideologies underlying the genre
- consider these films' audiences, and assumptions about those audiences.

Above all, my intention is to problematise the romcom, so that such films become new and strange again, and can therefore open up to analysis. This seems necessary since, although they seem easy to dismiss, romantic comedies can have a hold on us. Even hardened academics can be swayed by the patterns of gain, loss and recovery these films present so repeatedly. Whilst formulating the ideas for this book, for example, I saw *The Prince and Me* (2004), a fairytale romance set in Wisconsin in which gutsy medical student Paige (Julia Stiles) meets, derides and falls for upper-class Eddie (Luke Mably), never dreaming that he is so upper-class he is actually the Crown Prince of Denmark. When the paparazzi expose their romance, the lovers part and Eddie returns home; Paige follows to Denmark and agrees to marry him. At a grand state ball, however, she is excluded from an important diplomatic conversation and realises that this is what agreeing to marry the Prince means: always being in public, never having a say in political affairs. Paige calls off the engagement and flies back to America. Several months later, she finishes university top of her graduating class: Eddie is waiting to congratulate her. He agrees that Paige should become a doctor but must also marry him; having broken one tradition by letting an

American marry the Crown Prince, they might as well break another and let the future Queen have a job too.

While the trajectory of this romantic comedy is straightforward and fits entirely within the 'boy meets girl' outline to which Shumway refers, this bare-bones account does not adequately reflect *my* feelings on watching it. Putting myself in the place of *Sleepless in Seattle*'s Suzy for a second, I can relate that although the film did not make me cry, it did prompt emotions. As it seemed that Paige would give up her dream of being a doctor, I felt annoyed because, once again, the woman was making sacrifices for love. When she made what the film seemed to suggest was the 'right' choice, however, leaving Eddie and returning to university, I felt let down by the deviation from the norm. I wanted the two to end up together and I felt cheated that a romantic comedy could try to deny me the happy ending I expected from the genre, even though I wanted Paige to keep her career. When the actual ending, with the Prince's capitulation, unfolded, I felt it was unrealistic, implausibly tying up ends that would really have been left untidy in real life – but I was glad it was there.

This personal anecdote suggests that even when we know how a genre works, can tick off its expected components and predict in which order its events will occur, there can be something in the romantic comedy – whether it is escapism, comfort, wish-fulfilment or irony – which keeps audiences enjoying, and consuming, the films of this genre. This book sets out to interrogate what that something, or *somethings*, might be.

1   ROMANTIC COMEDY AND GENRE

Genre is a French word meaning 'type' or 'kind'. Thinking about film genres, therefore, employs ideas about different types or kinds of films. Deciding a film fits within a well-defined genre can be a way for film critics to dismiss it, since genre films are often assumed to be made in Hollywood, to strict guidelines, as mass-oriented products. To a certain extent, 'genre film' has as its implicit opposite the notion of the 'art film'; furthermore, genre films carry connotations flavoured with 'American, low-brow, easy', while assumptions about art films include 'European or independent, high-brow, difficult'. While genre critics have worked to unsettle these assumptions, contesting the idea that *all* genre films are inevitably 'popcorn movies', even genre criticism itself has culturally authorised some types of film, like westerns and gangster films, more than others. Romantic comedy is, arguably, the lowest of the low. Even a book setting out to review 600 'Chick Flicks' ends up admitting its own lack of taste:

> It's about time we confessed: we might love the great and the good, but we can also adore the cute and the ridiculously bad, as long as the leading man is handsome or the story – no matter how cheesy – makes us laugh, makes us cry, or makes us hot. (Berry & Errigo 2004: 1)

Romcoms are viewed as 'guilty pleasures' which should be below one's notice but, Jo Berry and Angie Errigo suggest, which satisfy because they provide easy, uncomplicated pleasures. I dispute this idea, however, and think that the appeal to audiences of such films is more complex, especially if the viewer is inhabiting a position where conflicting pulls of realism and fantasy are operating, as in my own reactions to *The Prince and Me*.

It is not only romantic comedies that are assumed to provide simple options for enjoyment: all genre movies seem straightforward because of their adherence to a recognisable formula. However, actually considering the elements of a genre and the expectations audiences have of different genres *critically* requires work and detachment. Since the 1970s film theorists have studied genre to problematise it, to question both what makes a film fit a genre and what 'genre' itself constitutes. Steve Neale and Rick Altman, for example, both importantly point to the intrinsic hybridity of genre films. While such multiple address, appealing to more than one audience sector through specific generic traits, can be assumed to be a characteristic of recent films, Neale demonstrates that hybridity has a longer history (2000: 2) and Altman notes that film marketing has always attempted to maximise audience appeal by proliferating the number of genres to which a film can belong (1998). These writers also indicate that most movies of whatever genre have a love story as one of their component strands, which can be highlighted or played down in the film's marketing.

Despite – or perhaps because of – the large numbers of such films which reach us in cinemas and at home every year, what actually constitutes a romantic comedy is seldom debated. Geoff King suggests that the common occurrence of both romance and comedy within many other film genres generates difficulties in appreciating what precisely constitutes the romcom: 'Defining romantic comedy as a clear-cut genre is difficult, because of the prevalence of both its constituent terms in popular film.' (2002: 51). Because these films seem so transparent (they are all about love, boy meets girl, and so on), precise definitions of their characteristics are not often attempted, with the result that a whole slew of films with very different topics of focus are given the same label. For example, some theorists, such as Mark Rubinfeld (2001), treat Cameron Crowe's *Jerry Maguire* (1996) as a romantic comedy, although the romance and comedy elements in the narrative seem overwhelmed by the accent on personal growth, sentiment and the establishment of a familial unit, rather than a couple.

Of course, film reviews and the works of theorists are not the only factors which delimit genre: production and marketing also provide sites where genre gets defined. Films come to audiences pre-packaged as generic products through marketing material, advertising and, eventually, as DVDs and videos. Romcom film posters, which are frequently reproduced as DVD covers, employ very consistent tropes to market their products, involving emphasising the central couple. Movie taglines, one-liners teasing the viewer by summing up or forecasting the narrative, also help direct audience assumptions about films, implying what genre is being employed and thus what outcome we can expect from a particular movie. For example, the tagline for *Kate and Leopold* (2003), 'if they lived in the same century they'd be perfect for each other', embodies the whole film's trajectory in just thirteen words: the named pair will meet through time travel and fall in love.

What qualities justify a film's inclusion within the romantic comedy genre? We will examine two Kirsten Dunst vehicles to try to assess them. *Bring it On* (2000) has Dunst as a high school student involved in a cheerleading contest and trying to win the heart of her best friend's brother, Cliff (Jesse Bradford), while *Get Over It* (2001) presents the same actor as a high school student involved in a school musical and trying to win the heart of her brother's best friend, Burke (Ben Foster). In my opinion, however, only the second of these is a romantic comedy. *Bring it On*'s main goal is to expose the problems of incidental daily racism affecting the lives of a troupe of black cheerleaders, a project it makes no easier for itself by following the events from the point of view of this troupe's main *white* rivals. In this film Dunst's character, Torrance, wants to win the contest and she wants to win the boy, but the contest is more important and the love aspect secondary, although this is the one she succeeds in. *Get Over It*, by contrast, clearly reveals that all Dunst's actions as Kelly are motivated by her love for Burke: while she does win a part in the musical, her goal throughout is to help Burke get over his old girlfriend and fall in love with her.

While both of these films are enjoyable enough, the variation in the emphasis on the central couple's romance is, for me, what excludes *Bring it On* from romantic comedy status, but confers it on the other Dunst vehicle. *Get Over It*'s emphasis on the aspirational love story seems a crucial factor; which leads to the following master definition of films within this genre:

a romantic comedy is a film which has as its central narrative motor a quest for love, which portrays this quest in a light-hearted way and almost always to a successful conclusion.

Note that, unlike David Shumway's 'boy meets girl...' formula, I do not suggest that the romcom is inevitably heterosexual; as the chapter on the radical romantic comedy of the 1970s and its recent successors will explore, however, despite several independent films portraying gay or lesbian relationships – such as *Go Fish* (1994), *Saving Face* (2004), *Touch of Pink* (2004) and *Imagine Me and You* (2005) – enjoying some audience and/or box office success, mainstream films have yet to follow this example.

Observe also that the above definition does not insist that romcoms are necessarily funny, although this might seem implicit in the term 'comedy'. I have used the word 'light-hearted' in the definition to signal that, while films of the genre generally end well and may elicit laughs along the way, I am also aware of the importance of tears to the romantic comedy. I want to acknowledge the mixed emotions these films commonly both depict and elicit.

Crying frequently occupies an important space in the narratives of the romantic comedy: as an index of the pain a lover feels when apart from the beloved, when rejected or lonely. As noted, crying – about love, romance and other romantic films – is central to *Sleepless in Seattle*. This film certainly conforms to the definition offered above in that its central driving device is a quest for love: both Annie and Sam are seeking the perfect partner. Comic moments occur on the path to the successful conclusion, when the two are united. But tears also play a fundamental part in the narrative: Annie, engaged to the steady and dull Walter (Bill Pullman), is both moved hearing Sam testifying to his love for his dead wife on the radio, and envious of the strength of his devotion, which she realises is missing from her own relationship. Tears are the result of both of these feelings and guarantee that, since she can be moved to tears by Sam's love, Annie merits its inheritance.

Noting the importance of tears in the romcom is an act of the active analysis of components within the genre's toolkit. For various reasons, considered in detail below, the romantic comedy is often perceived to be so obvious in its construction that its components are *not* analysed.[1] Furthermore, if critical attention is turned on the genre, often what would be legitimated as a *trope* (a recurrent element) in a genre which has some credibility, is dismissed as a *cliché* in the romantic comedy – even by its theorists (see for example King 2002: 58). Thus although the romantic comedy is one of the most *generic* of genres, heavily reliant on stock elements, personae and even dialogue ('I love you!'), the rudimentary machinery of the genre still needs investigation.

Generic elements

Three key components warrant consideration in assessing the internal attributes of film genres, descending from the surface deeper into the film: the visual characteristics, narrative patterns and wider ideology.

visual characteristics

We identify film genres by the kind of images found in them and, in turn, these images then become laden with a symbolism dependent on their genre: they become icons and their study within a genre dignified with the title of 'iconography'.

Colin McArthur, in a very useful article from his 1972 book-length study of the gangster film, provides a guide to looking at iconography within a genre which can assist the study of the romantic comedy. While subsequent work on the romcom has been alert to narrative shifts in tone and confidence (Henderson 1978; Neale 1992; Paul 2002), consideration of the *visual* aspects of the genre has not greatly advanced. McArthur suggests that iconography can include locations, props, costume and even stock characters (in the western these might be the barman, the saloon gal, the grizzly-bearded prospector). In the romantic comedy we will see such iconographic uses being made of settings (almost uniformly the contemporary romantic comedy now has an urban location), props (consider the repetition within the genre of articles associated with weddings, as well as flowers, chocolates, candlelight, beds), costume (the special outfit for the big date) and stock characters which most often include the unsuitable partner; here the characters who will be a couple by the film's end both start out with an unsuitable partner, illustrating the rightness of the central romance by being plainly wrong, as with Joe's (Tom Hanks) girlfriend Patricia (Parker Posey) and Kathleen's (Meg Ryan) boyfriend Frank (Greg Kinnear) in *You've Got Mail*.

narrative patterns

Films in the same genre share more than just key characters and props, however; they also utilise similar narrative patterns, both small and larger ones. For example, at the very smallest level there are the tropes, occurrences which happen repeatedly within genres. As McArthur notes, when we see a car coming down a dark alleyway towards someone in a gangster film, we recognise that the driver is going to try to kill that someone; a moment of peace often precedes a bloodbath, as in the scenes of quiet restaurants before a drive-by shooting. On a larger scale, another common generic pattern of the gangster movie is the rookie gangster's rise through the ranks, as he takes on bigger and bolder crimes, inherits the flashy dress sense, bigger guns and even the girlfriend of the big boss. At the level of the largest pattern, we anticipate a narrative arc displaying the rise and eventual fall of the mobster, a man who uses unlawful means to achieve the American Dream of riches and success.

Looking at the narrative patterns in this way, from the micro to the overarching level, the genre's key themes emerge. In gangster films the immigrant working-class character wants success but tries to achieve it illegally, so is ultimately punished by death. By contrast, the theme of the musical is that hard work and determination committed to the enjoyment of *all* is the best way for the *individual* to be happy and successful. When advancing precepts in this way (do not rob banks, do work hard in your community) narrative patterns go beyond themes, to indicate the ideology of the society creating them (Grant 2007).

The romantic comedy can also be seen repeating the same narrative patterns, from the wider story arc to the smaller tropes. As Shumway notes, the basic plot of all mainstream romantic comedies is boy meets, loses, regains, girl. Within this master pattern smaller moments also recur with regularity. The 'meet cute' was often employed in romantic comedies of the classic period in Hollywood: in this trope the lovers-to-be first encounter each other in a way which forecasts their eventual union. Billy Wilder, first a scriptwriter, then a director, is one of the foremost proponents of the 'meet cute'; he is supposed to have kept a notebook of ideas for cute meetings where the eventual couple would meet in a humorous, unlikely or suggestive manner (see Sikov 1998: 121; Chandler 2002: 80).[2] One of the most twee 'meet cutes' comes in screwball comedy *Bluebeard's Eighth Wife* (1938), which Wilder scripted: the couple first cross paths in a department store where he wants to buy only the top half of a pair of pyjamas and she the bottoms. The form of the meeting here assures the audience that although the couple may at times seem to hate each other, they will eventually reunite because they belong together as much as the top and bottom halves of pyjamas do.

Other frequently occurring tropes include the wedding derailed by one partner running away; the masquerade, in which one or both of the central characters pretends to be someone else; and the embarrassing gesture – this has one of the lovers submitting to public humiliation in order to prove that love is more important than dignity. Patterns which commonly occur in specific sub-genres are dealt with more fully in the chapters dedicated to them, while a further list of other suggested narrative tropes, with filmic examples, is given in Appendix B.

ideology
The ideology of a genre can both reflect and contest the anxieties, assumptions and desires of the specific time and specific agencies making the film. Gangster films generally tout the value of accumulating personal wealth, even while the genre tacitly acknowledges, through the lawless actions and ultimate fate of its gangster figure, the difficulties of achieving that goal. Thus these films underscore the American capitalist ideology of *legally* earning wealth, even while allowing audiences the vicarious pleasures of violating such legal strictures.

The basic ideology the romantic comedy genre supports is the primary importance of the couple. While this is usually the heterosexual, white couple, certain films from the 1990s onwards have attempted to widen the perspective to include gay and black couples. None, however, has tried to suggest monogamous coupledom itself is an outmoded concept; even *Annie Hall*, possibly the most radical film in choosing to deny the audience an ending with the couple's union, does not suggest the goal of finding one's true love is no longer desirable, merely impossible.

At the heart of every romantic comedy is the implication of sex, and settled, secure, within-a-relationship sex at that. Shumway's 'Exhibit A' of plots, with boy meeting girl, thus exists to dress up the naked fact that Western, capitalist society has traditionally relied on monogamy for its stability, as well as on procreation for its continuance. Shumway suggests that romance and marriage have opposing goals, which explains both real-life endemic dissatisfaction with the married state and the need for romantic comedies to end before the couple embarks on married life (2003: 21). The ideology of 'one man for one woman' can thus be seen to underlie these films in order to assure stability in Western, capitalist society; but films do not just reflect reality, they help to create it too. In giving the audience a high degree of closure with the happy ending in films of this genre, are romantic comedies benign, supplying an on-screen fantasy of perpetual bliss usually lacking in real life? Or do they negatively promote daydreams, making audiences long for a perfection which can, realistically, never be accomplished, leaving people dissatisfied with themselves and the relationships they do have? Perhaps both; a closer look at what the underlying ideology of the romantic comedy wants to foster in its audiences indicates why film studios go on and on providing fairytales for adults.

Although the current romantic comedy, with its awareness of divorce, biological clocks, myths about the shortages of single men and other simultaneous impulses towards and reasons against coupling, seems to have acknowledged the difficulties of finding true love, it nevertheless continues to endorse the old fantasies. This illustrates the strength of the ideological mandate towards coupling and the industries which depend on romance to make money. It may seem cynical to view romantic love as an ideal which supports capitalist consumerism, but the self-dissatisfaction such films breed can create a vulnerable space which advertisers have been only too quick to target. This fact is self-reflexively considered in *Kate and Leopold*. In a scene where the viewer can almost hear the iconography and generic tropes being ticked off the list (candlelight, romantic music, star-lit cityscape, slow dance) the couple (Meg Ryan and Hugh Jackman) enjoy a romantic dinner for two and she admits having never had much luck with men. When Leopold suggests perhaps she has not yet met the right one, Kate seems to step out of the film for an instant to comment on the whole romantic comedy genre and the industries it nourishes:

> Maybe ... Or maybe that whole love thing is just a grown-up version of Santa Claus, just a myth we've been fed since childhood so we keep buying magazines and joining clubs and doing therapy and watching movies with hip-hop songs played over love montages, all in this pathetic attempt to explain why our Love Santa keeps getting caught in the chimney.

Kate here testifies to her own consumption of items which both reinforce the ideas of romantic love (movies and magazines) and which she hopes will help to make her eligible for romantic love herself (health club membership and therapy, for a better outside and inside). The possibility of gaining romantic love just seems to be the bait that companies dangle before consumers in order to ensure we continue buying their products.

While most romantic comedies do not want to hint that the whole edifice of true romance might be as mythical as Santa, we as audience members, consumers and film scholars need to remember that big business relies on our urge to make ourselves loveable through the consumption of goods (make-up, shoes, underwear, grooming products, mood music, seductive dinners – and films). Hollywood is just one of these big businesses, and if we can accept that product placement in a film operates to sell more Coca-Cola and Nike products, why not also view the fantasy of romantic love as a product being no more subtly endorsed?

Exposing the tools used by a particular romcom can help examination of the underlying ideology the film reflects. While there are of course very sensitive micro-analyses of specific films,[3] there seems to be a prejudice against subjecting such fluffy trifles to intense critical scrutiny. Even people who make (and make money from) such films seem to acknowledge that the genre is less worthy than others, as a comment from Garry Marshall, director of *Pretty Woman* (1990) intimates: 'I like to do very romantic, sentimental type of work ... It's a dirty job but somebody has to do it (cited in Krämer 1999b: 106). While Marshall's comment can be dismissed as ironic, sarcastic or perverse, it still taps into an awareness of a prejudice against the 'romcom', an assumption of cultural lowliness, which needs to be considered and perhaps contested; this contestation is assisted by investigating the elements involved in the genre. Marshall's comment could equally apply to the work of analysing romantic comedies and their constituent elements, which simply has not been achieved in numbers comparable to works on other genres.[4] Let us consider some of the reasons which may account for their low status.

One aspect mitigating against these films is their seeming transparency, with films like *You've Got Mail*, *Sleepless in Seattle* and *Failure to Launch* (2006) appearing so naked in their project to get their men and women together by the last reel that it seems pointless to look for further motive or intent. The genre's simplicity thus deflects proper interrogation. Geoff King proposes this very transparency makes such films 'particularly effective vehicles for ideology. Their implicit "don't take it too seriously" helps, potentially, to inoculate them against close interrogation' (2002: 56).

Another criticism frequently levelled, particularly against contemporary romcoms, is that they repeatedly go over old ground without adding anything original to the mixture of traditional soundtrack songs, picturesque urban views and initially antagonistic, ultimately blissful male and female protagonists (Hampton 2004). Reviews regularly note the adherence to generic blueprints seeming stale now: American film-trade weekly *Variety*, for instance, found *How to Lose a Guy in 10 Days* (2003) conforming to 'trite formula' (Koehler 2003: 68); the reviewer for British critical magazine *Sight and Sound* agreed, feeling that the film's romance was 'underdeveloped' and its ending 'disappointingly cloying' (Wood 2003: 50). Repeatedly these two publications dismiss the narratives of romcoms as demonstrating a clichéd emptiness: condemning them for 'rote vacuity' (Matheou 2003: 48), for being 'slick but slight' (Felperin 2005: 26).

One further reason for the habitual critical contempt of romantic comedies may be its association with a female audience: 'romcoms' are popularly supposed to be 'chick flicks': the subtitle to Berry and Errigo's book of that title is 'Movies women love'. To emphasise the point, they include ten films they view as, by contrast, being more male-oriented, male-centred films.[5] Not only do romcoms usually present their stories from the perspective of their female lead character, detailing her feelings and thus privileging her within the film as the site of audience identification, but they are marketed to women, as the special summer 2006 Football World Cup tie-in advertising for *Imagine Me and You* made clear.[6] They are thus also assumed to appeal largely to women audience members, in the same way as were the 'Women's Films' of the 1940s (see Krämer 1999a and 1999b). These films – intense stories with strong, well-defined central female roles, about women suffering and sacrificing for love and family – were also critically downgraded until subject to a revisionist rescue mission by feminist film scholars in the 1980s (Modleski 1984; Mulvey 1986; Doane 1987); perhaps the current wave of critical investigation will do the same for the romantic comedy.

By assuming a largely female consumption of romantic comedies, scholars and critics alike disparage them, unconsciously or not; even now in the twenty-first century, women are still supposed to be more interested in gossip, relationships and clothes than important topics. Like fashion, which has long been held in low critical esteem and whose scholars have to work hard to justify their interest, romantic comedies may suffer from their association with female consumers despite the fact that, as the section on ideology indicates, these films do not actually speak solely to female interests and desires but are aimed more inclusively at both genders. The myth of perfect love appeals to both sexes, and the narratives of romantic comedy films themselves demonstrate that *both* women and men have to change and adapt to deserve love: if, annoyingly, in the masquerade plot which occurs as such a regular trope in this genre it is usually the man who is conning the woman, such films as *Pillow Talk*, *How to Lose a Guy in 10 Days* and *Lover Come Back* (1961) do demonstrate that, once the woman has discovered his deceit, the man has to change his ways in order to deserve her love again. In illustrating, too, that the romcom male has a nice apartment, designer clothes, an expensive music system and an enviable physique, the romantic comedy possibly encourages the men in the audience to remake themselves as fitter, more glamorous and possessing more and better consumer durables. Thus, regardless of the association of women audiences with the genre, the ideology which underpins it seeks to sell love, and products, to everyone.

As a final note, it should be emphasised that these various sub- and dominant genres are neither *all-inclusive* – that is, there were always romantic comedies being made at the same time as, for example, the screwball, which did not fit with the style of that sub-genre – nor mutually *exclusive*, in that it is possible to read *Pillow Talk* both as a sex comedy and as a romantic comedy. It should be recognised that screwball comedy was therefore not the *only* kind of romantic comedy in the 1930s, although it now seems to have been the most dominant; similarly, the sex comedy and the 1970s radical romance were not the only types of romantic comedies being made, but the cycles they belong to have emerged, over time, as the most influential to the genre's development. By contrast, the recent Neo-Traditionalist romantic comedy seems to be more numerous than influential; perhaps at this point in film history, when the romantic comedy seems forced to side either with the conservative narratives, like *Kate and Leopold*, or the more explicit gross-out films, such as *The 40 Year Old Virgin* (2005), the genre itself is waiting for a new impetus which will renew its energies and lead it in more interesting directions.

2   SCREWBALL COMEDIES

Studies of screwball comedies generally note the genre's inception in 1934, with the appearance of two films, Frank Capra's *It Happened One Night* and *20th Century* directed by Howard Hawks. Despite their differences in director, stars, crew and subject matter, these two films also share elements which have been taken as inaugurating a new strand of comedy with several specific historical and social motives for their emergence at this point (Harvey 1998: 287).

Screwball is traditionally assumed to have faded with the coming of the Second World War (Gehring 1988: 111; Byrge & Miller 1991: 1). I suggest that rather than having a fixed end, screwball comedy's popular tropes became integrated into the wider romantic comedy form. I will trace 'screwball' themes evolving into impulses in other film types, from the buddy movie of the 1970s right through to comedian vehicles in the early twenty-first century. Furthermore, classic examples of the screwball comedy anticipate some of the gender conflict characterising a subsequent manifestation of the genre – the sex comedy.

Screwball comedy: contexts

Although *It Happened One Night* and *20th Century* are usually hailed as the founding films of the sub-genre (Sikov 1989: 22; cf Harvey 1998), both lack certain characteristics which later came to seem indispensable; thus it is more the synthesis of themes and elements from these two films which produces the features we usually associate with screwball comedy.

It Happened One Night was an attempt by Columbia Studio to cash in on the popularity of a then-topical form of film, the 'bus picture' (Harvey 1998: 107) which featured a microcosm of Americans travelling together. By 1934 the cycle was established enough for *Variety* to praise *It Happened One Night* for its early abandonment of the plot contrivance:

> It starts off to be another long-distance bus story, but they get out of the bus before it palls and it is not handicapped by the restraint that locale always seems to impose ... [*It Happened One Night*] proves ... the best way to do a bus story is to make them get out and walk. ('Chic' 1934)

Combining the bus story with elements of comedy and romance, *It Happened One Night* inaugurated a new cycle of 'madcap heiress on the run' films, not all of which have subsequently been considered screwball comedies (as, for example, *The Bride Came C.O.D.* (1941)). The basic formula of such narratives was a rich woman meeting, being tamed and helped to mature by a poorer or seemingly socially inferior man, such social class commentary being especially appealing at a time when the nation was in an economic depression. *It Happened One Night* has a charm and freshness which contributed to its remarkable box office success, partially attributable to the unrehearsed tone of the dialogue; while this is very noticeable in the scenes between millionaire's daughter Ellie (Claudette Colbert) and newspaper man Peter (Clark Gable), especially as he recounts his rules for undressing, it did not become a standard feature of screwball, which often stresses qualities associated with written dialogue – speed, polish and wit – rather than the spontaneity which comes from improvisation.

Unlike the other film credited with beginning screwball, *It Happened One Night* does seem to be a genuine romantic comedy: the protagonists grow out of their carping and insults, realising that they love each other. This is expressed through Ellie's tears when she thinks Peter will leave without her, and tears are key in the romantic comedy. They have a much less prominent place in the sub-genre, however: no one really cries in a screwball film except in frustration. Certainly there are only tears of fury in *20th Century*, which, besides lacking that romantic love which forces the characters to grow up and stop bickering, is also without the class conflict found in *It Happened One Night*. Both protagonists, Lily Garland (Carole

Lombard) and Oscar Jaffe (John Barrymore), are wealthy stars of the theatre by the time of the main action, and while the beginning of the film indicates that Lily began life as poor shopgirl Mildred Plotka, there are references that Jaffe himself had equally humble origins. Class does not matter in this screwball comedy: it derives its energy solely from the personal clashes of the battling lovers rather than from any bigger categories the two might be taken to represent. The battling of the lovers takes overtly physical forms, with pushing, kicking and punching, not just word-sparring; while Peter may tell Ellie's father, in *It Happened One Night*, that she needs 'a guy that'll take a sock at her once a day whether she has it coming to her or not', there is no real feeling he will make good this threat. The protagonists of *20th Century*, by contrast, do not just threaten but gleefully act out their violent impulses: Oscar begins the hostilities when he 'helps' Lily scream in her first play by sticking a pin into her bottom. Lily keeps the pin: both as a token of Oscar's love and to remind her of the pain she owes him. What *20th Century* thus adds to the screwball formula is the idea that people in love will do everything they can to torment each other. This develops as a very noticeable theme within screwball comedy, although it is rarely enacted with such potential for real physical injury.

The emphasis on fast-flung insults and violence, either threatened or carried out, as a main trope in screwball seems the most vital difference between the sub-genre and the wider romcom genre. While many romantic comedies emphasise an initial antagonism between the female and male protagonists, they eventually modulate this dislike into loving behaviour, as insults turn to praise, slaps to caresses. The screwball comedy, by contrast, sustains the discord, using the energy of the couple's friction and mutual frustration to drive the narrative forward. In this way, the screwball comedy can provide for viewers a different kind of pleasure from that ordinarily offered by the standard romantic comedy which stresses (whether eventually, or throughout) the admiration and affection each half of the couple has for the other; in the screwball this affection is expressed through aggression.

While the romantic comedy thus oscillates between slapstick scenes and tender moments, the screwball comedy, fuelled by animosity, can direct its aggression into the humorous incidents it invents to punish the beloved, whether by embarrassment, insults, humiliation or real violence. As the psychiatrist tells Susan (Katharine Hepburn) in *Bringing Up Baby*:

'The love impulse in man frequently reveals itself in terms of conflict.' While the doctor means 'mankind' by his use of the word 'man' here, it should be noted that the aggressive, even predatory, *woman* is one of the most frequently occurring tropes of the screwball comedy. Some feminist film critics (for example Haskell 1974; Rowe 1995) have dubbed screwball a woman's sub-genre because of the frequency of the triumphant female. Others, such as Diane Carson (1994), see the threatened and sometimes acted-upon violence towards female characters in these films as a sign that they are not celebratory of the independent and active woman but, rather, are anxious about her and keen to punish her through the confines of the conservative narrative endings, which do often see women 'back in their rightful places'.

Synthesising elements from *It Happened One Night* and *20th Century* gives us: male and female protagonists, initially at war and by the end of the film maritally attached or re-attached; rapid-fire dialogue; a conflicting social class element; and a world turned topsy-turvy, the disruption of the characters' normal lives both exemplified in and carried out through the hectic chases and pratfalls which occur amidst settings and costumes of great elegance. How did these elements seem to have a resonance with audiences on their first release which powered screwball to a position of considerable, if short-lived, industry dominance and lasting influence?

To understand the rise of particular genres, we need to situate them within their cultural and historical contexts. In 1934 America was in the midst of the Great Depression, a countrywide slump in industry and finance which began with the stock market crash of 1929. Thousands of people were out of work, and many more faced losing their homes and health along with their jobs. Amidst all the retrenching of remaining budgets, however, one thing seemed to remain a necessity: the movies. Despite the perilous nature of many people's financial situations, film attendance did not decline in 1929, although by 1932 box office takings were down and several studios were in financial trouble, including Columbia, which went on to make, and be rescued by, *It Happened One Night*. What attracted people back to the movie theatres proved to be films which realistically portrayed the problems of the Depression, but with the characters ultimately triumphing over them, as with Warner Bros.' very popular backstage musicals, such as *Gold Diggers of 1933* (1933). *It Happened One Night* removes the audience for a time from its own experiences, to expose the arid upper-class world of privileged Ellie, but then brings her down to earth, and back to contemporary reality, by having her cross America with no money. The experience enriches her spiritually and emotionally and she grows as a person from her time spent without money; such a message – that poverty was morally superior to wealth – presumably offered some comfort to contemporary audience members.

Furthermore, the end of the 1920s also marked the introduction of sound to films, and this was as crucial for the development of screwball comedy as the background of the Depression. Before audiences could enjoy the particular pleasures of the screwball – insults, wordplay, personae, accents – cinema first needed to invent 'the talkies'. Another important factor responsible for the specific qualities of the screwball comedy was the active enforcement, after 1934, of the 1930 Production Code. This was a code of self-regulation adopted by the movie studios to pre-empt regulation from outside the industry, and for about thirty years ruled supreme in Hollywood, forcing on-screen married couples into separate beds and moralistic, conservative endings onto films (see Leff & Simmonds 2001). As the filmmakers began to realise the restraints they were working under, however, they began to find imaginative ways to exploit them, employing ambiguity to suggest and simultaneously disavow what was not allowed to be shown, including suggestive scenarios. This is potentially the reason why the screwball comedy has often been seen as a comedy of 'old love' (Henderson 1978: 10) or 'remarriage' (Cavell 1981; Shumway 2003): while, under the Production Code, a comedy could not display an active sexual relationship between an unmarried woman and man, it could hint at the continuation of a sexual relationship between a couple once married, now nearly divorced or separated. For example, *The Awful Truth* (1937) shows mutually suspected adultery resulting in divorce for Lucy (Irene Dunne) and Jerry (Cary Grant); both eventually realise they want the other back, and manage to reunite just before their divorce becomes final. By setting up a structure which has both the couple's reconciliation and their impending decree absolute proceeding against the clock in the final scene, the film teases the audience with the possibility that it might be daring enough to break taboos and permit un- (or at least post-) married sex, but neatly side-steps this at the end.

The term 'screwball' is odd enough for us to question how it arose as a description of a film type. Unlike, say, 'film noir', a title given to films which seemed to share certain characteristics long after the films themselves had been made (Borde & Chaumeton 2002: 1), 'screwball comedy' was a term used by critics, filmmakers and audiences while the films were appearing; *My Man Godfrey*, the film discussed in detail below, was placed in this sub-genre on its release by *Variety* principally because of the scatter-brained heroine: 'Miss Lombard has played screwball dames before, but none so screwy as this one' ('Bige' 1936). According to Ed Sikov, the notion of a 'screwball' is derived from baseball and was coined around 1934: a screwball was thrown fast and with a twist, in order to confuse the batter. The term 'screwy' had enjoyed common American usage for around fifty years, meaning first 'drunk' and then 'crazy'. So as Sikov says:

> by the early 1930s 'screwball' successfully brought together a number of connotations in a single slang and streetwise term: lunacy, speed, unpredictability, unconventionality, giddiness, drunkenness, flight and adversarial sport. (1989: 19)

These are the qualities making up the screwball comedy in its full incarnation: the characters act in unpredictable and unconventional ways, as if crazy or drunk; their language is pacy, their physical actions no less swift, with chases a common event for the symbolic representation of this violent form of love, as, frequently, the woman chooses and pursues her man and he flees from her. The term 'adversarial sport', with its connotations of competitive games, aptly describes the screwball attitude towards love: it is a game each combatant wants to win and is prepared to cheat in order to do so. With most screwball comedies neither side actually wins, the film ending instead with a benevolent draw in which both parties are reconciled.

Characteristics of screwball comedy

Screwball comedies can be seen to share various thematic characteristics:

- reverse class snobbery, so to be poor is somehow to be better. To be rich is to be out of touch, and being book-learned means needing a real education

- a major inversion or subversion of the characters' normality: this can be the heiress forced to live poor, a pauper suddenly gifted with money, a normally regulated life turned upside down
- role play: characters engage in masquerade, taking on different names, personae, accents.

Besides thematics, screwball films also share visual and aural elements. These include an overlapping style of delivery, with lines spoken rapidly, frequently by more than one character at a time; a well-written script, laced with barbed dialogue, insults and wordplay; and a blend of sophistication and slapstick – although screwball characters move in an elegant world with beautiful art deco sets, costumes and high tone settings, nightclubs, hotels and mansions, they still whack each other over the head, tear their clothing and fall over.

It Happened One Night exemplifies reverse class snobbery as a trope. The film begins by revealing how spoiled heiress Ellen (Ellie) Andrews is: 'imprisoned' on her father's yacht because he does not approve of her marriage to King Westley (Jameson Thomas), she refuses to eat and throws a tray of food onto the floor, before jumping overboard and swimming to shore. Ellie's naivety, assuming she can make her way with limited funds, is exposed as a rich person's malaise: she is forced very quickly to learn the true value of money in Depression-era America. What makes her bearable as a character at this point is her energy: in choosing, literally, to jump ship in order to rejoin the man she loves, Ellie is wrong (as the man is a stuffy snob) but redeemable. She just needs to meet the right man, and soon does, in the person of Peter Warne, a cynical newspaper man. Peter joins forces with Ellie and they travel across country together, during which time she learns about life in the real world. The phoniness of rich people is mocked, and cosy proletarian values are celebrated instead; the scene on the bus where everyone is singing together acts as a counterbalance to the moments where we see Ellie's father shouting at his minions. Harmony can only prevail where everyone is prepared to join in, the film seems to suggest; while there may still be problems in life (the bus crash, the sneaky blackmailer) these can be faced better as a community. The rich man and his daughter, before her alternative education begins, are morally bankrupt, while the poor people lack only money, not heart. ·

Peter proves himself the proper match for Ellie by attempting to educate her about street-smart ways (he steals carrots for her and, when she finally accepts them, her action tacitly apologises for her waste of food at the film's start), and by acknowledging, however grudgingly, that there are things she can do well too (such as use her shapely leg as bait to trap a passing motorist whilst hitchhiking). Above all, although Peter frequently lectures Ellie about the proper way to act, the important point for their future as a couple is that they learn about things, and enjoy being, together. The scene where they pretend to be married in order to evade detectives forecasts that they will be a couple, as their ability to play spontaneously together confirms they deserve to be.

The reverse class snobbery which pertains throughout the film also permits the narrative to indulge in slightly risqué scenes with the excuse of realism. Since motel rooms cost $2 each per night, and the couple are too poor to afford two rooms, they have to say they are married and share a room together. Despite the Hays Code which came into force in the same year as *It Happened One Night*'s production, there are still a number of elements in the film which are suggestive of sexual desire as well as of romantic intimacy between the pair. For example, Peter undresses in front of Ellie, the camera lingers on shots of her underwear and, most noticeably, in a later bedroom scene, the camera captures the woman's very obvious physical desire for him. Ellie goes around the blanket he has hung as a modesty curtain in the middle of their shared space, traversing the line between her domain and his as a silent proposition. Peter sends her away – reluctantly – because she is still married to King Westley.

Because Peter has educated her, when she returns home Ellie cannot settle back comfortably into the empty life she led before. Preparing to re-marry King Westley, Ellie looks nervously about her as she walks down the aisle, as if all the luxury and riches surrounding her are a prison. In a scene very influential to romantic comedy, Ellie finally chooses Peter at the moment she is about to re-take her marriage vows to Westley and, running across the lawn with her wedding train streaming out behind her, not only embodies the 'madcap heiress' persona but also the 'runaway bride'. In needing to meet and be tamed by the 'right man', not coincidentally from a lower social echelon, Ellie also seems to be running away from the tyranny of the upper classes towards egalitarianism, as well as sexual fulfilment.

The film is radical enough to end on Ellie running out on one wedding rather than displaying her entering into another one with Peter, thus preserving the free-wheeling liberty being on the road gave them, rather than the confinement of being within the family. The pair return to the motel where they had enjoyed romantic intimacy before: this time the modesty curtain is ceremonially removed, with the suggestion of all other barriers to the couple's sexual union going with it too.

The same strain of reverse snobbery is visible in *Bringing Up Baby*, in the film's obvious contempt for Professor David Huxley's (Cary Grant) book-derived learning, but this film manages to turn the idea of reversion into a major theme, aptly exemplifying the concept of inversion operating within the screwball comedy. Kooky Susan Vance destroys the entire life of David Huxley, an archaeologist and dinosaur expert, and the film urges the viewer to celebrate this destruction, since his values are so hopelessly skewed. David's achievements, when the film begins, are a fiancée he is about to marry and a dinosaur skeleton he is about to complete. However, the fiancée, Alice Swallow (Virginia Walker), is sexless, passionate only about ancient history and denies the importance of a honeymoon, while David's archaeological interests are literally as dry as dust, the dinosaur skeleton as ossified as his own sexuality.

Just as Ellie, though rich, needs to be taught the real value of money, David, though bookishly clever, needs to be given a true education. Money and class notions are forgotten about in *Bringing Up Baby*, as both heroine and hero seem to inhabit a world far removed from Depression-struck America. While he works in a museum he has ample time off for golf games which might net him more funding, and Susan is a scatter-brained heiress whose luxurious apartment testifies to her more-than-comfortable standard of living. While *It Happened One Night* underlines the class connotations of its plot, and *Bringing Up Baby* ignores any such issues, both films make the character positioned as the teacher (Peter of Ellie, helping her survive on the road, and Susan of David, providing lessons on fun) also importantly teach the other about sexual desire.

Bringing Up Baby's main theme is topsy-turvy, another of the key elements of the screwball: the main character's life is suddenly subject to subversion, as everything he has known, worked for and valued is swept away and destroyed. The film expects the viewer to see this is much for the best; allowing the agent of destruction simultaneously to save David, the film conforms to Richard Gollin's description of the sub-genre's main impetus:

> the screwball comedies of the 1930s ... paired a conventionally repressed person with an unconventional opposite, apparently flea-brained but in fact instinctually shrewd, who altogether overturns various plans and thereby makes possible a future together laced with impulsive vitality, sportive fun. (1992: 127)

Significantly, and not mentioned here by this male critic, it is usually an anarchic *female* who undercuts the pomposity of the stuffy male. Here the films do not content themselves with just mocking the man, seeking to deflate his self-regard, but more importantly display the need for his rescue from arid and sexless pursuits. It is possible to see popular Freudianism, just then beginning to affect Hollywood, at work here, and to map psycho-analytic terms onto the characters: the repressed person can be seen as the Ego, subjected to assaults from a freer soul, the Id, who wants to liber-ate the hero's unconscious desires. There is a sense that the stuffy partner wants to be free, but has let responsibilities build up until there are too many things hemming him in to walk away. The violence committed upon his regular life is thus necessary to free him.

Because *Bringing Up Baby* was made in 1938, when the Hays Code was fully established, the script cannot overtly announce that David is miserable because he is sexually repressed, but thanks to popular Freudian symbolism (David has a missing 'bone') the point is conveyed to the viewer. Furthermore, Susan's inversion of David's usual orderly life is clearly revealed to be based on her desire for him: after the film's introduc-tory 'meet cute', which has Susan accidentally claiming first David's golf ball, then his car, her actions become consciously directed to foiling his attempts to leave her. To do this, Susan is prepared to lie, cheat, steal, kidnap and generally behave irresponsibly and with enormous sponta-neity and gusto. This is demonstrated in the scenes where she lures the unsuspecting archaeologist to her side to prevent him attending his own wedding.

The film contrasts the two women in David's life as he talks to each in turn on the telephone, not only in their costumes – Alice's is formal, neat, prissy; Susan's is gorgeously floaty, idiosyncratic and sensual – but also

Figure 1: The uptight Miss Swallow from *Bringing Up Baby*...

Figure 2: ... and the rather more sensuous Susan Vance

in the tenor of the conversations with each. Although he seems initially hostile to Susan ('Oh, it's *you!*') and obedient to Alice, the former's manipulation of the encounter reveals a different aspect of David's personality. Susan summons David to her apartment to help her capture a leopard. When he refuses and she then falls over, having tripped on the phone cord, he assumes she has been attacked by the leopard and she, spontaneously manipulating the situation, screams down the phone so he will come to her rescue.

Clearly Susan is an anarchic force; quick-witted, she lies to and manipulates David, making him fear she has been hurt, in order to get him for herself. This spontaneity is the complete opposite of David's arid life and what perhaps unconsciously attracts him to her: certainly he rises to the occasion, becoming a hero, setting out to rescue her. While thus adhering to the screwball trait of inversion, the film clearly also demonstrates the typical generic blend of pratfall and slapstick elements with glamorous sets and costumes.

By the end of the film, David has been kidnapped by Susan and taken to Connecticut, forced to wear women's clothing, dig up dog bones, sing to the leopard and been arrested and thrown in jail. In the last scene, Susan arrives to announce she has secured the sponsorship David needs, but then, even as the pair seem to confirm their love, she accidentally destroys his most important dinosaur skeleton just as she has methodically destroyed everything else in his life. The film thus maintains the screwball comedy concept that love turns your world upside down, but the resultant chaos is more fun. Susan's destruction of David's dry and sexless existence is something he should thank her for, as she has taught him – though messiness, breakages, insults and sexualised role-playing – to enjoy life.

The thematic elements of reverse class snobbery, inversion and role play are found across a range of screwball comedies; to examine how these common traits work together in a film, I will now turn from analysing the elements separately to examining their combination within one film.

Screwball comedy case study – My Man Godfrey

While not as frequently discussed as *Bringing Up Baby* or *It Happened One Night*, *My Man Godfrey* clearly fits into the sub-genre, exhibiting its trademark visual, verbal and thematic elements. Like the former film it introduces an anarchic, elemental, female force to a dignified male victim, and observes the resultant subversion of his normality; like the latter it includes a class element which opposes the rich and spoiled heiress with the down-to-earth man of the people. Unlike those films which either enforce the class element (*It Happened One Night*) or ignore it altogether (*Bringing Up Baby*), it cheats a little with the class radicalism it seems to be setting up, because Godfrey (William Powell) turns out to be from a family as well-off as Irene's (Carole Lombard). While, then, the film adheres to the screwball idea of romantic love as possessing an element of 'adversarial sport', with battling lovers, the match of Irene and Godfrey is not as subversive as that of either Ellie and Peter, or Susan and David, since neither does the genuinely lower-class man teach the spoiled heiress some important lessons, nor does the scatter-brained female release the stuffy male through exasperating play from the bonds of his arid life.

With its blend of slapstick action and sophisticated milieu, *My Man Godfrey* is very obviously a screwball comedy; but how romantic is it? As noted above, many of the films considered to be 'classic' screwball comedies seem to be more concerned with punishing and humiliating the beloved than celebrating and praising her/him. The energy driving such films as *The Awful Truth* and *My Favourite Wife* (1940) is conjured by the opposition of the lovers and their commitment to outwitting each other, which accounts for the films' ending at the point of the tentative reconciliation of the protagonists: ironically, while this is ostensibly what is desired and worked towards, once achieved the energies of the film dissipate and the stories close hurriedly. *My Man Godfrey* fits with this tendency in the screwball, as Irene tries to cajole or con Godfrey into loving her; the motivation for this too seems to be less romantic love and more overt sexual attraction, another noticeable trend within screwball. Irene is very clearly so smitten with Godfrey she invites him into her bedroom, follows him about the house in a daze and becomes piqued when he will not be her 'protégé', a refusal motivated by his own sense of self-worth.

Although Irene and Godfrey do marry at the end of the film, there is no sense that the pair love and need each other, as there is in *It Happened One Night*, a successfully *romantic* screwball comedy. Irene gets a minister to marry her to Godfrey in the nightclub, telling her future spouse with a giggle, 'Now stand still, Godfrey, it'll all be over in a minute' as the film closes. Certainly Irene wants Godfrey, but perhaps more because he has

Figure 3: Irene Bullock gets her man, Godfrey

always denied himself to her than for any other reason. She does not seem to have grown up or learned anything, as Ellie clearly has. Instead, Irene continues to demand what she wants and when she engineers her marriage to Godfrey his acceptance seems based more on resignation than desire. In this way the film seems rather embarrassedly to endorse her way (marriage, sex) rather than his (dignified platonic friendship) simply because of generic obligations. Inevitably the film has to end with the hero and heroine together, and it does so, but it should be noted that the couple are not in a clinch as is traditional, nor engaging in sexual play in the dark (*It Happened One Night*) nor even perching above a collapsing dinosaur (*Bringing Up Baby*) but with the man clearly shackled to his fate, looking anxious as the screen fades to black and his new wife laughs in triumph.

My Man Godfrey employs the usual screwball milieu of mansions and nightclubs as the backdrop for the film's action, and the usual mixture of sophistication and slapstick obtains too, with one memorable scene where the usually self-contained Godfrey, drunk, still attempts to serve dinner with his usual dignity. While the visual tropes of the sub-genre are intact, then, with the art deco-inspired sets, the film is less successful in grafting the social commentary element frequently found in screwball onto the narrative.

The film seems initially to tackle this point very clearly with its location of the hero in the down-and-out Godfrey, employing the screwball tropes of reverse class snobbery and inversion by taking a derelict out of the dump and letting him live amidst luxury. The film clearly refers to Depression-era politics in making the scavenger hunters go looking for a 'forgotten man' (see Appendix A). *My Man Godfrey* is thus tapping into a contemporary hot topic by having its hero reclaimed from the city dump. However, it ultimately fudges its political thrust by having Godfrey turn out to be not a soldier or worker consigned to the dust-heap through the Depression, but a former rich playboy inhabiting the dump through choice. Unlike the real forgotten men, Godfrey came from and could return to luxury and high status. He is thus more self-forgetting than forgotten in the topical sense, and this creates a crucial difference in the political weight the film's narrative can claim. While *My Man Godfrey* may, like *It Happened One Night*, posit the rich as empty-headed, spoilt children, setting up a clear opposition between the ignorant and selfish Bullocks and the noble, intelligent and always dignified Godfrey, it then abandons the inherent social thrust of this contrast by having Godfrey actually belong to an equally rich family. Since Godfrey has rich relatives, the opposition the film establishes between the butler and his employers is not one of poor versus rich, but old money versus parvenus, a far cry from the democratic impulse it seems, at one point, to wish to endorse.

Besides attempting to employ reverse class snobbery, the film also uses the other common screwball themes of inversion and masquerade, although, again, its success is somewhat limited by its choice of characters. Godfrey's 'normal' life in the dump is inverted when Irene swoops down on him and he finds himself, within 24 hours, as live-in butler at the Bullocks'. Life in the dump, moreover, was an inversion of his former life, as a rich idle playboy. The narrative sets up a scenario in which it can satirise the wealthy by implying that their humble-born butler has more manners, intelligence and courtesy than they do and is thus in a perfect position to teach them to be better people – far from being their inferior, he would be thus their superior, as they were learning from him. However, by making Godfrey really their social equal, the film loses this satirical potential. The fact that other forgotten men encountered in a second visit to the dump are also courteous, dignified and polite, even amongst the filth in which they live, is furthermore thrown away when Godfrey points out to his friend Tommy (Alan Mowbray) 'that little man ... that's Bellinger of the Second National [Bank]'. The city dump seems to be entirely populated by formerly rich men; while there is potential for a dig here against a society which ungratefully forgets businessmen as soon as they make a mistake, the fact that there seem to be no permanently poor men living in the dump, only ex-rich ones, saps the satirical spirit of the film, making it whimsical and slightly surreal, where it could have been pointedly political. Humans left on the ash-heap of life seem less pitiable, and society as a whole less guilty of abandoning them, if they have all chosen, like Godfrey and Bellinger, to be there.

Godfrey's masquerade as the perfect manservant is thus not too radical a pretence: he has the perfect manners of a gentleman because he *is* one. In using the masquerade motif, *My Man Godfrey* attempts to employ the common screwball theme, but neither Godfrey's own disguise nor the pretence occurring in the relationship with Irene provides the same type of rejuvenation of character found in other screwball films. Unlike the spontaneous role-playing of Peter and Ellie, which unites them in a fantasy of marriage forecasting their eventual union, Irene and Godfrey do not play together as equals. When Irene pretends to be ill so Godfrey will not leave her, he sees through the deception immediately and places her, fully dressed, in the shower, drenching her. The pair do not use role-playing as an occasion to act as a unit against others, as Peter and Ellie and David and Susan do, but in opposition to each other, Irene feigning illness to keep Godfrey, he feigning humble birth to keep her at a distance.

While thus employing the common visual and thematic elements identified with the sub-genre, *My Man Godfrey* performs its own modulation of these elements; unlike *It Happened One Night*, which can be read as both a screwball film and a genuinely romantic comedy, the film seems less interested in the love relationship between the central protagonists and more with the surrealist elements of the plot. Certainly the energy generated in the early scenes of the scavenger hunt where goats, spinning wheels and goldfish are jostled by mink-clad debutantes and men in evening dress is never matched in the scenes where Irene and Godfrey interact, and the film's conclusion seems more interested in the conceit of a nightclub erected on the site of the old city dump, employing its former

Figure 4: Gregory LaCava's surreal *mise-en-scène*

residents and attracting New York high society, than in the wedding which unites the pair.

Evolution of the screwball comedy

As noted earlier, while most writing on the sub-genre agrees its formation in 1934, authors seem to have different notions of how long 'true' screwball persisted, with various dates given for its demise.[1] Most theorists agree, however, that the form faded during the years of the Second World War (see Britton 1986; Krutnik 1990; Byrge & Miller 1991; Everson 1994; Harvey 1998). During their heyday, what myths were the screwballs tapping into that account for its popularity? Perhaps the motif of inversion, applied to everything from sexual and behavioural norms, to traditional values, as in the valorisation of the poor over the rich, could be seen as a filmic representation of the real fact that the Depression had removed certainties. By suggesting this inversion could offer pleasure to the protagonists, the films might then be seen as reassuring worried viewers that topsy-turvy could be good, energy-renewing: in other words, offering hope.

If the films can be seen as encouraging their protagonists and thus their audiences to indulge themselves in play and fun in the suspension of daily constraints, this message came to seem, as America approached entry to the Second World War, to be out of step with contemporary thinking, the frantic chasings, pratfalls and glib barbs between two wordy and frequently wealthy protagonists now too trivial, inappropriate for a more serious world. As Frank Krutnik notes:

> The 'battle of the sexes' was overwhelmed by a more tangible and other-directed warfare and, in the early wartime years in particular there are indications across a range of Hollywood films of a reluctance to validate romance as an all-important issue when there were 'graver matters' at stake. (1990: 70)

Certainly the few screwball comedies attempting to use the war for humour have been seen as disastrous: while there are fans of Ernst Lubitsch's *To Be or Not to Be* (1942) (see Everson 1994: 216), Leo McCarey's *Once Upon a Honeymoon* (1942), which brings screwball stalwart Cary Grant to occupied Europe and, at one point, commits him to a concentration camp, cannot manage successfully to blend screwball's usual funny accents and role-playing with patriotic speeches about freedom, and violence that is no longer verbal or at least personal and between battling lovers, but armed and on the scale of genocide (Britton 1986: 49; Krutnik 1990: 70 n.3; Harvey 1998: 271; but cf Wood 1976).

Some writers believe that common screwball traits persist in films into the 1950s (Harvey 1998: 287; Wood 2001: 16) and, as will be seen in the next chapter, the use of slapstick amidst sophisticated splendour was a key part of the pleasures offered to audiences by the Battle of the Sexes comedies, along with the now-standard romantic comedy trope of the protagonists who share a physical attraction only equalled in force by their loathing for each other's personalities.

Whether or not the sub-genre did actually disappear, however, its habitual absence by the 1970s was marked enough for *What's Up, Doc?* (1972) to make use of it in its advertising: the film's tagline was 'A screwball comedy. Remember them?' *What's Up, Doc?* relocates *Bringing Up Baby* from upstate New York to San Francisco and makes play out of the city's extreme hills and bay in the climactic comic chase. *What's Up, Doc?*, however, extends the difference between the uptight academic male and the freewheeling spontaneous woman through foregrounding their ethnic differences, an element of comedy which has been more influential in subsequent films which are not romantic, due to continuing racist notions about miscegenation. *What's Up, Doc?* overtly presents kooky Jewish Barbra Streisand shaking up uptight WASP Ryan O'Neal; presumably the star power of the former was enough to overcome squeamishness about the resultant mixed-ethnicity relationship, or perhaps in the 1970s American audiences were more prepared to accept Jewish/Christian lovers, as *Annie Hall* would also later present. The trope of the uptight white man and the relaxed, funny, cool, ethnic other, as found in *What's Up, Doc?*, can be seen taken over into buddy movies such as *48 Hrs* (1982) and reversed with a certain irony in the *Lethal Weapon* series (beginning 1987), where rather self-consciously it is black Danny Glover who has the normal life and white Mel Gibson who is the anarchic force disrupting it.

The ideological message of this evolution of screwball needs investigation, as the inevitable aligning of the woman or black person with the thoughtless, elemental forces of nature versus the white man as representative of civilisation, thought and neurosis is patronising and sexist, racist or, at times, both. For example, in *Bringing Down the House* (2003), the ideology of race is used to underline and support the sexism so that Queen Latifah's child/woman, Charlene, becomes representative of the more relaxed, hip, happy-go-lucky black people. Redoubling racist stereotypes onto sexist ones, Queen Latifah is presented as such a force of anarchic nature that she ruins/enriches not only the restricted life of the uptight white male lawyer Peter (Steve Martin) but also affects the lives of his daughter and son, his Jewish friend and a stuffy English client too. All of the transformations are observable in the film's finale which pits a supposedly street-cool Peter against black underworld gangsters. The inheritance from screwball comedy of a willingness to improvise, to undertake role play and accents, marking the newly-made screwball hero, is seen here. However, because of continuing social taboos within American society about interracial romance, the obvious screwball conclusion, which would be to have Peter and Charlene form a romantic couple, is not permitted. Instead Peter wins back his (white) ex-wife Kate (Jean Smart) and Charlene gets Jewish Howie (Eugene Levy).

Figure 5: Peter shows off his street style in *Bringing Down the House*

While it could be argued that the film is attempting to problematise the notions of race operating in contemporary American society, simultaneously the film can also be posited as being patronising and racist, not mocking racial stereotypes but endorsing them and in fact using them to underline and support the sexism potentially inherent in a film form where a man with everything but *joie de vivre* has his world shaken up by a woman with nothing but. This pairing of gender and class differences is not new, but can be traced back through the sub-genre, even to its origins in *It Happened One Night*, where the elemental force changing Ellie's privileged and ultimately shallow and unhappy life is significantly a *lower-class* man. While the performances of the "kooky" half of the dyad can work to resist confinement by cliché – as with Gable or Streisand, or Queen Latifah, who in *Bringing Down The House* seems so charismatic that her Charlene exceeds the common stereotype of streetwise, hot black Mama – tacitly attesting, as screwball films do, that the (white) privileged have everything except life and the black/Jewish/female anarchic force has nothing but life removes the need for "everything" – material goods, rights, education – to be redistributed, because after all, "they" are actually better off than "we" are. This is not to condemn all screwball comedies or the films influenced by them, but just to ensure that as we watch them we are alert to their underlying messages and the ideologies they are tapping into.

3 THE SEX COMEDY

While the screwball comedy delighted in exhibiting male and female characters clashing and striking sparks off each other, the sex comedy took this
theme and implied such clashing was inevitable: all men and all women
were perpetually in conflict because nature had set them up – or society
had inspired them – with different goals. My definition of the sex comedy
highlights both the sexual and adversarial aspects of the sub-genre:

> The sex comedy pits woman against man in an elemental battle of
> wits, in which the goal of both is sex. Only the timing and legitimacy
> of this differs from gender to gender, with women wanting sex after,
> and men before or without, marriage.

While the sex comedy emerged at a precise time, the assumption that this
sub-genre, like the screwball comedy before it, existed for a number of years
but then vanished is not borne out by actual examination of films. It seems
instead that core elements of these sub-genres are more long-lasting than
this strict chronology implies, managing to endure because their defining
elements were absorbed into the main genre, the romantic comedy, after
the impetus behind the sub-genre itself disappeared. In other words, while
by the mid-1960s changing sexual mores made the sex comedy seem old-
fashioned and inappropriate to the new 'swinging' times, its visual and
thematic elements were not abandoned along with the narratives, but
incorporated into the mainstream romantic comedy. Even the narratives
themselves could be recycled. For example, here is a synopsis: two profes-

sional rivals, a hard-working woman who prepares for each new project meticulously and a man who gets by – and wins – each time by relying on his personal charm and charisma, meet and seemingly dislike and actually are attracted to one another, until, after getting riotously drunk, they wake up married. Horrified at what they have done they split up, before realising, at the end of the film, that they truly love each other and belong together. This outline fits both the sex comedy *Lover Come Back*, and the mainstream romantic comedy *Laws of Attraction* (2004), illustrating that while over forty years may have passed between them, recurrent tropes from its past sub-genres still occur within the contemporary romcom. It should be noted that the later film is in no way a homage, neither evoking the style or stars of the earlier film (as Peyton Reed's 2003 film, *Down With Love* attempted to do); instead, the motif of the battling lovers and the stereotyped oppositions which accrue to its female and male leads (uptight vs. spontaneous; hard working vs. hard living; sexually prudish or inexperienced vs. promiscuous) are enduring because they provide the energy to drive the story line. As with the screwball comedy, much audience pleasure derives from seeing the couple openly fight and insult each other, underhandedly plot to foil the schemes of the other, and secretly yearn to fall into bed together. The sex comedies suggest the intense animosity between the pair will guarantee a passionate sexual relationship by the film's end.

Contrary to the view of the sex comedy which allows it to flourish only for a decade from the mid-1950s to mid-1960s, I think there has always been a strand within romantic comedy where much of the pleasure and energy of the film is derived from the couple's efforts to *resist* being a couple, to deny their fitness for each other and the inevitability of their union. For example, the battling lovers in *20th Century* fight and scheme as well as sleep together, and the viewer is encouraged to realise the pair deserve to be together because they are awful in the same ways. However, there are modulations to the comedy in different historical contexts: the explicitness of the sexual element waxes and wanes depending on the societal mores of the time of production. While there were many silent comedies which dealt, in a racy manner, with the subjects of sex, marriage and adultery (see Musser 1995), the sex comedy as studied in this chapter emerged at a time when a range of factors meant sex, sexuality and desire were hot topics and, for the first time since the 1934 adoption of the Production Code, some discussion of these topics could be openly attempted.

While the sex comedy appropriates and exaggerates the animosity of the central couple derived from the screwball comedy, unlike the screwball the sex comedy has received much less critical attention; thus, although it is easy to find a list of films traditionally regarded as screwball, it is much harder to find a similar canon of classic sex comedies or an understanding of the common elements shared by films of the grouping. Alexander Walker's article, 'The Last American Massacre: Rock Hudson & Co.' (1966), written while the sex comedy was still an active sub-genre, provides what is probably still the best overview of this type of film, despite his obvious view that such movies represent low cultural product. While looking down on such films, Walker does recognise the importance of the *mise-en-scène* to the sex comedy, and usefully notes several recurrent tropes (feigned impotence, 'alcohol and immersion' (1966: 222–3)).

However, Walker makes the fundamental mistake of assuming the women in the sex comedy are always out to guard their virginity and thus are anti-sex; in aligning this manipulative sex-shunning virgin with star Doris Day, Walker also contributes to the wrongful yet persistent assumption that Day 'always played a virgin', when her portrayal of this stereotype was actually limited to just one movie, *Lover Come Back*. Although Walker did not inaugurate the dismissal of Day as virgin, his article has been highly influential on subsequent writers about both sex comedies and Day (for example Krutnik 1990; Fuchs 1997; McCallum 1999). As the detailed analysis of *Pillow Talk*, below, will indicate, however, Day's star persona is not inevitably read in terms of stale virginity, nor is her sex comedy heroine invariably anti-sex.

Examination of the film in its historical context relieves Day's character of the burden of an oppressive allegiance to her maintained chastity which subsequent writers have tried to fasten on her: as with the screwball comedy, the specific historical period in which the sex comedy emerged was vital to its development. Returning the films to their originating context more fully enables the films, their elements and arguments, to be understood.

Sex comedy contexts

Three key events which occurred in 1953 contributed to the development of the sex comedy. The first was the publication, in August, of Alfred Kinsey's report on *Sexual Behaviour in the Human Female*. Kinsey had previously, in 1948, issued a similar report on male sexual behaviour and, while the findings of this report had provoked a strong media response, this was as nothing besides the hoopla resulting from his study of women. Even the idea that women *had* sexual behaviour worthy of study was shocking to contemporary audiences; imagine then the mingled shock, outrage and prurient excitement generated by the news that his report suggested half the women in the country were having unmarried sex! While the statistic – indicating that of the 5,940 unmarried white 30-year-old American women whom Kinsey interviewed about their sexual experiences, just over half were not virgins – would not be startling in today's society, in 1953 it was received as a bombshell.

Kinsey's results, published to enormous media response, directly opposed the contemporary ethos of the 'double standard'. This was an unwritten law implying that men were supposed to have pre-marital sexual experience, and women were not. Kinsey's research revealed that half his sample had ignored this dictate and had lost their virginity before marriage. Not only was this 50% revelation startling to a society which assumed women obeyed its injunction to refrain from sex until after marriage, it also prompted further anxieties. The key point was that Kinsey's revelation *was* a revelation, people realising that not only might assumptions about chastity be incorrect, but also that there was no definite way to know. 'Bad girls' and 'good girls', contrary to traditional belief at the time, were not easily distinguished by eye.

Besides Kinsey's explosive report, a further publishing innovation also contributed to the new climate of anxiety and excitement over sexuality, both female and male. The magazine *Playboy* first published in November/December 1953 was dedicated to enjoying a range of sensual pleasures; while other contemporary men's magazines such as *True* and *Modern Man* endorsed traditional outdoor pursuits such as shooting and fishing, *Playboy* was happy to pursue a resolutely urban line, celebrating indoor activities of which sex was only one:

> We like our apartment ... We enjoy mixing up cocktails and an hors d'oeuvre or two, putting a little mood music on the phonograph and inviting in a female acquaintance for a quiet discussion on Picasso, Nietzsche, jazz, sex. (Anon. 1953: 1)

Playboy's ethos was, as here suggested, importantly not only predicated on sex but on a range of consumer goods and cultural experiences being marketed to masculine audiences: the stereo, records, alcohol, the bachelor pad. *Playboy* devoted much of its monthly issues to articles listing must-have items which, it implied, would increase both the bachelor's pleasure in his apartment and his chances of luring women there for sex. This emphasis on consumables is picked up in the mid-1950s sex comedies, and is significant in targeting both women (as romantic comedies from the 1990s onwards clearly do) *and* men, the playboy hero of the sex comedy's key films displaying his good taste and culture in the art and furnishings of his bachelor pad, along with the very modern conveniences which turn an apartment into a lair, as considered below.

One final event of 1953 which contributed to the sex comedy context was the release of the film *The Moon is Blue*, which contained the first use of the word 'virgin' in a legitimate, non-pornographic film, since the imposition of the Production Code. Based on a 1951 stage play, the plot revolved around the attempts of two men to seduce Patty O'Neill, a very outspoken young woman who proclaims her sexual inexperience to anyone who will listen. *The Moon is Blue* was denied a seal of approval from the Production Code Administration, largely because of its racy narrative and frank (for the time) language, but director Otto Preminger managed to get it exhibited anyway. While not the first film to be released without a PCA Seal, it was the first major film to advertise its own independence and thereby generate audience interest. Due to the success of the film and audience members' evident willingness not to be protected in their viewing by the Production Code Administration, the power of this body began to be regularly challenged by filmmakers and thereafter rapidly declined. By 1956 it had been revised into a format which 'lifted all remaining taboos except nudity, sexual perversion and venereal disease' (Leff & Simmons 2001: 225) and lasted in this weakened form until 1966.

These three separate occurrences together created the context for the sex comedy: *Playboy* introduced the persona of the urbane purchasing bachelor, inhabiting a luxurious lair to which he would invite women; the success of *The Moon is Blue* in challenging the PCA meant filmmakers were emboldened to discuss sexual topics in films more frankly; and Kinsey had made such discussion and depiction imperative with his announcement that women actually had sexual desires and impulses, just like men. With

Playboy thus creating the setting for the comedies, *The Moon is Blue* inaugurating their language and Kinsey's report providing the narrative, as well as the character of the new desirous young woman, mainstream Hollywood had simply to pick up these pieces and use them.

From around 1954 for about a decade, then, the sex comedy enjoyed popularity at the box office in this form. It began to decline in the mid-1960s when the idea of readily available reliable birth control, in the form of the contraceptive pill, made films based on the withholding or postponement of sex because of the implicit fear of unwanted pregnancy seem outmoded. The sex comedy would have to change to survive the new moral climate which no longer assumed 'nice girls' would insist on marriage before sex. This assumption, despite Kinsey's 1953 revelation of many women's discounting of the double standard, was the dominant one of the sex comedy from the mid-1950s onwards: the genre was not yet willing to present a young woman successfully shedding her virginity as the subject of a comedy. Instead the films chose to tease and lead on the audience with the promise of sex and then refuse to deliver until the end-reel marriage. By the mid-1960s, however, this insistence on delayed sex felt out-of-step with the times. The shift in attitudes can be charted across two examples of films starring starlet Sandra Dee. *Come September* (1961) details the attempts of Tony (Bobby Darin, Dee's real-life husband) to seduce her. Dee's character, Sandy, is fully a match for him, however, and reveals herself as the manipulative virgin of popular culture by determining to reel him into marriage by alternately dispensing and withholding her favours. By 1966's *Doctor, You've Got to be Kidding!*, however, the Dee character is no longer holding out against seduction: the film begins with the young single girl about to give birth to a baby in hospital, while three young men beg to marry her – the implication being that any of them could be the baby's father and thus tacitly acknowledging that not only did young women have sex, but they also had the potential to have serial relationships.

A final thought about definitions of this sub-genre, before moving to examine the films' common characteristics: although such films are called 'sex comedies', their date of production and targeted general audience ensures there is going to be very little actual sex in them. Although the severely-weakened Production Code now permitted the discussion and narrativisation of sexual topics, it still successfully forbade the visualisation of them. There would be no sex *enacted* in the sex comedy of this

period: where sex is implied, there are still discreet fade-outs or visual met-
aphors. Also, partners are usually married to each other, even if this only
occurs eventually: for example, in *Sunday in New York* (1963), it is apparent
that Adam (Cliff Robertson) has been having a sexual relationship with his
girlfriend whom he finally asks to marry him at the end of the film.

The word 'sex' in the generic title might be seen to be doing double
duty there: to indicate the participants in the skirmish (sex as gender) and
to denote the battle field (sex as sex). The 1950s–1960s sex comedies
could in fact be called 'Battle of the Sexes comedies' since this more accurately encapsulates their dynamic. Although the particular tropes and elements found repeatedly in sex comedies do not disappear entirely outside
this timeframe, but remain as impulses which can readily be seen in contemporary romantic comedy films, the introduction of the contraceptive pill
in the early 1960s in America, and its acceptance within media awareness
within the next few years, did mean that by the end of the 1960s the terms
of the sub-genre had changed and it no longer seemed realistic to centre
an entire plot on the 'would they or wouldn't they?' question. Ironically, as
soon as it could legitimately show what it had always been about, the sex
comedy seemed to lose all interest in doing so.

Characteristics of the sex comedy

Just as the screwball comedy had well-defined elements which the films
in the group share, the sex comedy shares conventions of narrative and
visual patterning, not only across the originating mid-1950s phase, but
observable in later examples, up to the present day. While several of the
ideas and tropes have, like the battling lovers, been absorbed into the
wider romantic comedy genre, other elements remain which recur when
the main thrust of the narrative is about sex and the idiots it makes of
otherwise rational people. In this way the sex comedy appears to make the
romantic comedy seem more realistic, more earthy, in dealing with bodily
urges rather than emotional impulses, but the comedy in the film is still
derived from demonstrating that people suffering under either intoxication
– passion or emotion – behave like idiots.

Several of the thematic characteristics common to the sex comedy are
also present in the screwball, but in the later films are given significant
revisions in their handling. These themes include:

- disguise and masquerade – unlike the screwball use of this motif, here the adoption of an alternative persona usually has both a sexual motive and sexual component; it also leads to the smaller sex comedy convention of 'truth through lies'
- a 'hierarchy of knowledge' in which *he* knows more than *she* and we know more than *either*
- reversions, inversions of the 'natural order'

Sex comedies also employ some micro-tropes, including: the protagonists who hate at first sight; tricks, insults and embarrassments; a set piece of an anti-marriage speech; and visual characteristics which include the apartment setting and glossy costumes. Music will often blend a romantic style for the intimate moments with a comedic score, reminiscent of the kind of music played to accompany silent slapstick. An instance of this typical musical style can be found in *Lover Come Back* when the Doris Day character discovers she has been deceived: instead of hearing her own moan of mingled fury and disappointment, the audience is given a trombone 'Mwaaaaaaaah!' which undercuts the expression of her emotions, making comedy out of her misery.

While critics studying the sex comedy of this period have been quick to see that woman is inevitably pitted against man in an elemental war, with the goal of each destroying that of the other, it is an over-simplification to state their opposing goals are sex for the man and marriage for the woman; the films of the time indicate that women want sex too. The real opposition lies in *when* this sex is to be achieved since the man is supposed to want sex without marriage and the woman to want marriage before sex. Because the woman is then supposed to insist marriage must take place before intimacy can be enjoyed, and will not willingly either succumb without this, or even be anywhere near a man who flouts his permanent opposition to it, as many of the sub-genre's playboys do, there neatly arises the need for subterfuge to bring the couple together. Thus the sex comedy relies on the idea of masquerade for its main plot mechanism.

Whereas in the screwball the romantic couple would have their fitness for each other confirmed by their ability to play together spontaneously, in the sex comedy the adoption of a new persona is carried out by one of the protagonists against the other. Usually it is the man who puts on a different person with the adoption of an accent and the creation of a new name; when the woman masquerades as someone else it is often to take in a female rival, rather than to get back at the male, as in *Move Over Darling* (1963), where Ellen (Doris Day) pretends to her ex-husband's new wife Bianca (Polly Bergen) that she is a Swedish masseuse. As mentioned above, the usual motivation and terms of the masquerade are both sexual: frequently, in order to bed the woman, the man will pretend he is too courteous, or shy, or even impotent, to do so. This theme is observable across the sub-genre: Rock Hudson's virile playboy Jerry pretends to be shy scientist Linus in *Lover Come Back* in order to seduce Carole (Doris Day); Joe (Tony Curtis) in *Some Like It Hot* (1959) pretends to be both saxophonist Geraldine and impotent millionaire Junior to seduce Sugar (Marilyn Monroe), and Curtis reprises both the masquerade and the impotence scam in *Sex and the Single Girl* (1964) where his target is played by Natalie Wood. *A Very Special Favour* (1965), towards the end of the sex comedy's main cycle, has Rock Hudson again play a man feigning a series of sexual problems – irresistibility, insatiability, impotence, homosexuality – which the film implies is a rising scale of seriousness caused by the resistance of the woman of his choice.

Even when the pretence is not sexual in nature, its motivating force is: in *Come Blow Your Horn* (1963), Alan (Frank Sinatra) has so many girls he has his young brother take one, Peggy (Jill St John), off his hands by pretending to be a powerful movie producer. Sex is the reason Alan wanted the girl around, but with the arrival of two others, he has to offload her onto his brother, so *he* then gets to enjoy sex with her. While Peggy is not 'punished' by the narrative for having sex, as she would have been in former years because of the dictates of the Production Code, she is clearly being exploited by the brothers, and the audience is meant to see her own willingness to have sex to secure (as she believes) a film role means she deserves what she gets, being passed around from man to man as she, the good natured but dumb bunny, attempts to manipulate them. Significantly in this film, as in so many others of the period, it is the 'good' girl, the one who does not give in to the man's seductive wiles, who ends up marrying him. While Connie (Barbara Rush) is seen to respond to Alan's caresses and clearly desires him too, her ideas about morality and self-respect dictate that she wants sex with him within a committed relationship. When he refuses to accept her terms Connie ends the relationship and will not see him until he capitulates to her ultimatum. This is the inevitable end of the sex comedy of the period: the man's masquerades and plots are (usually) exposed and the woman, who has not stooped to such levels, is rewarded for her patience by getting the man the way she wants him: legally. Because so much of the energy generated in sex comedies derives from the suspicion and fear of marriage, and the scheming and plotting to get sex outside of its confines, the films tend to present the marriage only within the very last few minutes of the film, so that maximum time can be given to resistance to it and only the very minimum to its celebration.

While films of the same broad period could, outside the sex comedy, relax the hierarchisation of the innocent good girl over the experienced bad one, as for example, *North By Northwest* (1959), *The Apartment* (1960) and *Breakfast at Tiffany's* (1961), which all feature sexually experienced heroines who end up with the right man at the end, the sex comedy itself rigidly maintains this distinction, as least as far as its main characters go.

These two patterns observable within the sex comedy – that the good girl, not the sexually available one, gets the man, and that marriage is inevitably the end of the story (and hence of any freedom, wit, humour, spontaneity and sexiness occurring within it) – clearly relate to the contemporary assumptions of the society producing these films. While Kinsey had informed the public that women did want sex, the films manage to dispel the anxiety this provoked by assuring everyone that, regardless of this, they were still prepared not to give in to their desires but would wait for a man who would marry them first – the maintenance of the double standard. In *Come Blow Your Horn* it is not Peggy who gets Alan, but chaste Connie. The sex comedies attempted to reassure audiences that, despite Kinsey's bombshell, nothing had really changed.

The masquerade theme is so fundamental to the sex comedy that other characteristic elements of the sub-genre derive from it; the idea of 'truth through lies', the instituting of a 'hierarchy of knowledge' and reversals of the usual order of things all take their impetus from a scenario in which the male protagonist adopts an alternative persona. The first of these concepts has endured into mainstream romantic comedies when such films employ the role-play or disguise motif: this is the idea that in becoming a different person, the hero becomes a better one. In *Tootsie* (1982) Dustin Hoffman's character Michael, who has masqueraded as Dorothy, realises he 'was a better man ... as a woman than I ever was ... as a man'; similarly the hero of the sex comedy has his personality enriched by the pretence as well as being rewarded with experiencing the true love he had never known in his 'real' self. The man, pretending to be someone, or more accurately *something*, else, ceases to be the sexually aggressive he-man he has habitually been acting, and while his more passive, respectful self is invented as a ruse to trick the woman into bed, its real effect is not her capitulation, which is always prevented at the last minute by some plot invention, but his improvement, becoming nicer, more loving, by the insights he has gained while not being a wolf.

Another element many films of the sex comedy share is the establishment of a 'hierarchy of knowledge'. David Bordwell and Kristin Thompson (2003: 84) speak about this in relation to the detective film in the classic Hollywood tradition, in discussing how suspense and expectation are used to draw in the audience: it relates to what awareness the characters and viewer have of the unfolding events. While in the detective film the audience will often see the hero finding clues, or working things out, he is usually in a higher position within the hierarchy of knowledge than the audience – that is, he knows more about what has happened and thus, when he reveals who the villain is, we can expect to be surprised. In the sex comedy, however, the audience is usually at the top of the hierarchy: the man, assuming a different persona as a scam, knows more than the innocent woman who is the object of his plotting, but the viewer knows more than either of them, thus creating the suspense and humour of the situation. For example, in *Sunday in New York* the audience knows, as journalist Mike (Rod Taylor) does not, that his new girlfriend Eileen (Jane Fonda) is both a virgin and rather weary of this status, as well as knowing he is a wolf and her sexual innocence therefore really is at risk.

The woman's revenge on the man who has deceived her provides a satisfying inversion of the narrative's direction and squares matters between them, so with both punished and humiliated, they can finally forgive each other. In later versions of the sex comedy, however, the plot is sometimes not uncovered at all. In several films featuring Doris Day (including *The Thrill of it All* (1963) and *Where Were You When the Lights Went Out?* (1968), the masquerade which tricked the woman is not discovered by her to be a falsehood and the film ends instead with her character still believing in the truth of the pretence, an unsatisfyingly imbalanced conclusion.

The inversions which form a common element of this type of romantic comedy further illustrate prevailing assumptions about appropriate behaviour for men and women. While in the screwball the trope of comedic inversion suggested, with the reversal of the everyday, a liberation from the crushing routine which the protagonists had allowed to dominate them, in the mid-1950s sex comedy inversion is employed for humorous effect, thereby suggesting the norm is actually correct. As a comparative example, we can consider the reversals which occur across different decades in *Bringing Up Baby* (1930s) and *Lover Come Back* (1960s). In the former, Susan Vance destroys David Huxley's ordered and regular life, his wedding and his reconstructed dinosaur skeleton: the film wants us to appreciate that this destruction is both necessary and therapeutic as it releases him from the boredom and sexlessness of his existence. In *Lover Come Back*, however, the reversals come about not through the anarchic actions of a character who chooses to ignore societal rules and make up her own, but through the manipulations of calculating playboy Jerry Webster, who decides to punish his advertising agency rival, Carole Templeton, by making her fall in love with him and tricking her into giving him her virginity. To do this he invents 'Linus', a scientist successful at his own research – he has a Nobel prize – but hopeless with women. This results in Carole having to assume dominance within the relationship: teaching him to dance and swim, taking him out to dinner and paying for it, buying him new clothes and getting him a haircut, then, finally, trying to seduce him in her apartment. The scene culminates in what is supposed to be the biggest reversal, when, in the course of a conversation about *his* virginity, Carole chases 'Linus' around the room. The point is that the film finds these actions funny because it is the woman, not the man, performing them, and this goes for the teaching and the presents as well as the seductive dinner for two. The humour lies in the incongruity of the events, the reversal which creates the man's passivity and the woman's action, because, it is assumed, men are not passive and women not in charge. Such a restrictive view of gendered behaviour indicates contemporary societal assumptions about the two sexes, as well as the anxiety raised by reports like Kinsey's which implied these assumptions could not be substantiated. The film insists on the natural passivity of women precisely because it is worried that such passivity might be wrongly assumed. Significantly, reversion for comic purposes has remained one of the strands of the sex comedy persisting into the mainstream romantic comedy: its occurrence should prompt the question of what norms are believed to be so basic that their reversal is *inevitably* humorous.

Further micro-tropes occurring in the sex comedy include protagonists who hate each other (often unseen, thus enabling the masquerade plot and permitting the man to woo the women in another persona); tricks, insults and embarrassments being forced onto the woman, usually, in the course of the romance (as when, in *Lover Come Back*, shy 'Linus' manages to manipulate Carole into taking him to a strip show) and, as a recurrent visual reference, the setting of the bachelor's fantasy apartment. Often the heroine will also be permitted a fabulous apartment, but this, while spacious and attractive, is not a *lair*. The male's apartment by contrast is equipped for seduction: music swells, lights dim, doors lock and the couch even converts into a double bed, all at the flick of a switch. Alexander Walker notes that the emphasis given to the fantasy apartment makes it practically another character in the movie (1966: 228): in *Come Blow Your Horn*, *Under the Yum Yum Tree* (1963) and *How to Murder Your Wife* (1965), the details of the lavish set up go beyond mere backdrop to provide character insight, suggesting an element of neurosis in the insistence on sexual conquest. In the last of these films the narrative further hints that the wife deserves murdering because her feminine possessions disrupt the total masculinity the apartment represents.

Often a set piece of a ritualised anti-marriage or anti-woman speech also operates within this form of comedy. 'Why would I want to get married?' demands the playboy hero, the audience knowing all the while that he will do so before the end of the film. His capitulation by the end is supposed to make up for his outspokenness during the contra-monogamy rant, as found in *Pillow Talk*, *Come Blow Your Horn*, *How to Murder Your Wife*, *Phfft* (1954) and *The Tender Trap* (1955). Again, in *How to Murder Your Wife* the anti-female message is given even more room than usual: the denunciation of marriage occurs early on, when the hero Stanley (Jack Lemmon) goes to a stag party which seems like a funeral until the groom stumbles in to announce the bride-to-be has jilted him. The all-male gathering erupts into cheers, and the groom himself plays 'Happy Days are Here Again' on the piano. At the end of the film when Stanley is, falsely, accused of murdering his vanished wife, he admits the crime but convinces the all-male jury they must acquit him if they have ever wanted to do the same to their own wives: they let him off. Though Stanley's wife is not dead, the violence done to her by the film seems real enough since her life is deemed disposable.

Sex comedies present the bachelor viewing marriage as a tragedy, implying that only emasculated men, men who have given up trying, want to get married. However, while the films very clearly suggest all healthy men, whether bachelors or already caught, hate marriage, it is a false parallel to assume the women in these films hate sex. In fact, the man's sexual campaign and likelihood of success would seem to have everything in its favour once we look at the couples involved in the fighting, since the woman can also clearly be seen desiring sex, as in *Lover Come Back, Under the Yum Yum Tree, Sex and the Single Girl* and *How to Murder Your Wife*. While it is often assumed (Walker 1966: 235; Krutnik 1990: 71 n.6) that these comedies inevitably pit a determined virgin against an experienced seducer, examination of the desirous females in the films reveals that women *are* willing to have sex, within a loving and honest relationship. It is the lack of honesty and respect, not the prospect of sex, which sends them running, as discussion of *Pillow Talk* demonstrates.

Sex comedy case study: Pillow Talk

Pillow Talk is a sex comedy which manages to blend the energy of its sub-genre, derived from the antagonism between the main characters, with a romantic tone more often employed in the mainstream romantic comedies. The film not only permanently changed the star personae of its two main actors, Doris Day and Rock Hudson, but also inaugurated a series of bright, glossy sex comedies which, for all their tameness by current standards, seemed daringly racy at the end of the 1950s and the beginning of the 1960s. It makes use of then-topical allusions – to the attempts at moon launches, to being in analysis – which made it seem very of-the-moment and also employed then-newly adapted split-screen technology, intro-duced to deal with wide-screen space, to juxtapose the couple as they talk on the phone and, rather suggestively, imply visually they are sharing a bed or a very large bath. The split-screen device also works to forecast their eventual coupledom when, for example, Jan's appearance drives a wedge between one of Brad's many girlfriends and the playboy.

Both critically and financially a success, *Pillow Talk* has one major, very topical, plot point: it depends on a problem belonging to a precise and short-lived historical moment – the lack of telephone lines. *Pillow Talk* hinges on the sharing of a 'party line' – one line, although with two differ-

Figure 6: *Pillow Talk*'s split screen can let Jan and Brad bathe together...

Figure 7: ...or forecast how Jan will wedge herself into Brad's life

ent numbers, which is shared by different subscribers or 'parties'. The film hangs its entire plot on the friction between the two sharers caused by the man using the telephone all the time, so the woman never can.

Pillow Talk makes use of some of the thematic and visual elements common to sex comedies, using disguise and masquerade, both revolving around sex: in order to get it Brad has to seem to renounce it. Wolfish Brad becomes courteous, gentlemanly 'Rex' to seduce Jan, but acting out a more passive, less grabby masculinity has an effect on him as well as on her: he finally manages to relax and fall in love. Being less aggressive than he normally is reveals the better, truer version of Brad which always had the potential to develop, and thus bringing in the other linked sex comedy concept of reaching the 'truth through lies'. The disguise plot also enables the establishment of a hierarchy of knowledge, which adds to the film's humour by creating irony and suspense. Again the man knows more than the woman, but we also know more than him, as the audience can hear both their thoughts.

Significantly, however, *Pillow Talk* does not demonstrate the theme of reversals in the sexist manner which the later sex comedies present. In this film the narrative does not delight in making fun of Jan (and thereby women in general) by making her do all the work towards her sexual undoing, as in the loose follow-up, *Lover Come Back*; in treating Jan as an experienced mature woman, rather than the determined spinster of some later sex comedies, *Pillow Talk* does not presume her pursuit of Brad is a reversal of the natural order but a testament to their mutual passion. The film plays more fluidly with ideas about oppositions which demonstrate that, for all their fighting, Jan and Brad are more like each other, and thus better fitted as a couple, than they are like other characters in the film. To this end the film contrasts them not so much with each other – since both are successful and enthusiastic about their jobs, moneyed, urban, well-dressed – but with people around them, setting up oppositions not between Jan and Brad but between Jan and her maid Alma (Thelma Ritter), Brad and his best friend Jonathan (Tony Randall), Jan and the other girls whom Brad romances, and even Brad and himself as 'Rex'.

The ultimate device used to underline the sameness of, and therefore the fitness of the match between, Jan and Brad, is the internal monologue. While, at the beginning of the masquerade, humour is generated through Brad's calculating awareness of the 'Rex' effect coupled with Jan's innocent praise of his alias – 'It's so nice to meet a man you can *trust*...', soon this develops into both characters scheming to get the other into bed. Both Jan and Brad are seen behaving one way and commenting internally about their real, contrasting, feelings: indeed, Jan is given an entire sung monologue, as the pair drive down to the country for the weekend, in which she outlines her desires:

Hold me tight and kiss me right, I'm yours tonight
My darling, possess me!
Tenderly, and breathlessly, make love to me,

My darling possess me!
Near to me, when you are near to me, my heart forgets to beat!
Stars that shine, make love divine, so say you're mine
And my darling possess me!

That this song is coupled with Jan subtly putting the moves on Brad – snuggling up to him, getting him to put his arm round her, moving ever nearer – creates humour, since her outward appearance implies innocent proximity, while her internal words reveal her hidden, sexual, agenda. Given this passionate declaration, it seems wilful that critics (Dowdy 1973: 183; Fuchs 1997: 232) have so often portrayed Jan as either frigid or a virgin: as the song and Day's performance illustrate, she is desirous of sex with Brad.

Pillow Talk also features some of the other smaller tropes common to the mid-century sex comedy, including the protagonists who seem to hate each other but are destined to be together, the fabulous bachelor apartment and the anti-marriage speech. With this, the film allows Brad the chance to criticise the emasculation he feels marriage and family life bring:

> Before marriage, a man is like a tree in the forest, he stands there, independent, an entity unto himself. Then he's cut down, his branches are cut off, he's stripped of his bark and thrown into the river with the rest of the logs. Then this tree is taken to the mill. And when it comes out, it's no longer a tree. It's the vanity table, the breakfast nook, the baby crib and the newspaper that lines the family garbage can.

Later, when he realises he loves Jan, Brad's arms are full of logs for the fire in front of which they have been making out: the film subtly suggests he has realised monogamy (the chopping down of the tree) does not have to be the end of passion, but can incorporate it (fiery flames = passionate sex). Here the anti-marriage speech and its antidote are both rendered wittily and symbolically, and pertain to Brad's anxieties about commitment, rather than being directed against marriage and women themselves. This is a very rare occurrence in the sex comedy, and one of the reasons why *Pillow Talk* is such a *romantic* example of the sub-genre.

Figure 8: Brad's branches are cut off

Evolution of the sex comedy

As noted, the particular context in which the mid-century sex comedy flourished ended when the contraceptive pill became an accepted fact within the media. With no reason left for women to be guarding their virginity – which is what the sex comedy had come rather monotonously to involve – a sub-genre depending on sex being talked about, plotted and lied for, but never actually enacted, lost its impetus. While it is true that this occurred at the same time as the increasing media profile of the Woman's Movement resulted in new awareness of societal pressures on women to conform to what now seemed outmoded ideas – pre-marital chastity, the sanctity of home and family – and the counter-culture movement criticised such institutions as marriage and family as bourgeois, it would be wrong to suggest the sex comedy declined in the format outlined above simply because it was rejected for being sexist. Portrayals of women in the later 1960s comedies are no more sympathetic or enlightened because of the feminist movement; in fact, emphasis on the female characters begins to decline.

The new 'swinging sixties' era permitted a continuation of the idea of deriving comedy from sex. However, once the emphasis changed from men trying to con women into bed to men succeeding at this, the problem facing the hero became not the overcoming of her resistance but the marshalling of his resources, with so many willing women now around. It seems very significant that the comedies of the later 1960s and early

1970s devote much more space and attention to the man; it is as if women were only in the earlier sex comedies to say no, and once the imperative for this was removed they lose their importance in the narrative. Certainly the women in later comedies tend to proliferate and the emphasis shifts from being about sex to being about him and some other endeavour on his hands which is frequently interrupted by demands for sex by this slew of glamorous though hardly differentiated women. The most popular genre of all films in the mid-1960s was the spy movie,[1] both straight treatments of the theme and the spy spoof which takes the sexual component and glamorous settings of the sex comedy and blends them with the emphasis on the hero of the spy films. Thus James Bond spoofs such as *Our Man Flint* (1966) and *The Silencers* (1966) featured heroes surrounded by attractive, over-sexed 'bunnies' and presented their central male with just one mate at the end of the film only to have her replaced by another in the inevitable sequels.

Some filmmakers did choose to examine the concepts of 'free love' and sexual libertarianism being touted as new and widespread in the late 1960s; *Bob & Carol & Ted & Alice* (1969) satirises the wealthy Californians who make up its two central couples, seeing how their adoption of trendy free love teachings and a doctrine of total honesty about sexual matters complicates their lives rather than freeing them from false ideologies. Overall, however, the sex comedy went into decline once it could actually begin to display what it had always talked about; even *Bob & Carol & Ted & Alice* only hints at the actual depiction of sex. While the comedy of sex proved to be a topic filmmakers did not seem often interested in exploring for some years, in the 1980s a new evolution emerged: the teen sex comedy, in films such as *Porky's* (1982) and *Losin' It* (1983). Here film narratives could return to the notion of the taboo against sex and use it as the motor to drive the plot forward: sexual initiation provided the opportunity for revisiting the 'will they or won't they?' idea. Lowering the age range of the characters from mature men and women, as in *Pillow Talk*, to young teenagers, allowed the narratives to provide a number of reasons why sex was not being achieved, such as family pressures, lack of self-confidence, religious and moral codes, and eventually fears of AIDS and other sexually-transmitted diseases, as well as why there was such an imperative towards achieving it – peer pressure, willing partners, raging hormones (Shary 2002; 2005). This evolution underwent a resurgence from the late 1990s with films like *American Pie* (1999), and sex, the acts and paraphernalia thereof, began to be openly used as the central topic of comedy in Hollywood films such as those by the Farrelly Brothers (*There's Something About Mary* (1998); *Me, Myself and Irene* (2000)). Finally humour is derived from the awkwardness, clumsiness or mess humans incur when they want to have or are having sex, when they are trying to abstain from it, as in *40 Days and 40 Nights* (2002) or have never had it, as in *The 40-Year-Old Virgin* (2005) where the sexual misfortunes and near-misses of hero Andy (Steve Carrell) provide the laughs.

These later films do not represent a return to the sex comedies of the mid-century, however, because they lack the essential opposition of male and female driving those films. This theme can be more readily found in the contemporary mainstream romantic comedy, where the first part of a film will often detail the battle of the sexes embodied in two individual protagonists, before moving to a more romantic comedy narrative in the second part. In *How to Lose a Guy in 10 Days*, for example, the protagonists Andie (Kate Hudson) and Ben (Matthew McConaughey) act out the battle of the sexes as each lies to and schemes against the other, generating much energy and humour in the narrative. The opposing schemes of each – she has taken a bet she can get him to be her boyfriend and dump her in the ten days of the title, while he has taken a bet he can get any girl to love him – stand in for the eternal opposition of male and female. Because this is 2003, the woman's scheme is not to be married but released and, because the film is wittily aware of its sex comedy antecedents, his scheme is not to bed her but to make her fall in love with him through his display of restraint.

The film employs the stock elements of the sex comedy, with the masquerade on both sides, as he pretends to be a gentleman, not rushing her into bed, and she sets out to be the perfect catch before then changing into the girlfriend from hell. Interestingly, the balance implied by their both having a masquerade is subtly undercut by the fact the film only employs the familiar 'truth through lies' motif for him: Ben learns to be a better, truer person by being a false one, actually getting a chance to get to know Andie as a person by delaying bedding her, and thus falling in love with her. But Andie's masquerade has her pretending to be horrible – this does not reveal a truer, better her but a fake one, a persona she sheds as soon as she can. The film also establishes a hierarchy of knowledge but again departs from the 1960s sex comedy by having the audience always know more than both the two characters: *we* know they both have an ulterior motive while they each only know of their own deceit.

How to Lose a Guy in 10 Days also uses the trope of reversals, when it sets Ben up to make Andie fall in love, rather than into bed, with him. It also gives a small homage to the importance of the bachelor apartment by highlighting the lair-like qualities of his place and then detailing how Andie maliciously transforms its seductive masculinity by importing frilly fabrics, cuddly toys and cupboards full of feminine toiletries and cosmetics. Again the assumption the audience brings to the film is that, both despite and because of the vehemence with which the central couple fight, they will form a couple by the end of the film, their shared aptitude for plotting, deceiving and masquerading guaranteeing they belong together.

Towards the end of the film, when the couple realise they love each other and they discover each has been lying to the other, the film shifts away from the energy of the battle of the sexes mode to the tearful component of the contemporary romantic comedy. In this film, as in the mid-century sex comedies, it is interesting that the end of fighting tends to mean the end of the story, since once the reconciliation takes place and the fighting stops, both the humour and the dynamism of the film seem to fizzle out. The drive of the sex comedy from whatever period is generated by the fighting, insults and scheming, and once the couple love each other sweetly the films have to end. While the narratives assure us that the intensity the pair brought to fighting will translate into passion in the bedroom, the fact that these films inevitably end on the reconciliatory kiss leaves room for doubts over whether a sustained relationship will ever be able to evoke the same excitement as did the skirmishes of the fighting stage. The films of the next chapter bravely looked at these doubts, producing narratives which unsettled the conventions of the entire genre – for a time.

4   THE RADICAL ROMANTIC COMEDY

After the gradual decline of the sex comedy Hollywood seemed to lack a dominant form of the romantic comedy for several years. As the 1970s progressed, however, it became clear that a new sub-genre had emerged, one which departed in several radical areas from the traditional characteristics of the genre. This evolution of the romantic comedy was influenced by its societal context, just as the screwball and sex comedy were, the particular climate of American society in the late 1960s and early 1970s affecting the way in which romantic comedy of this period developed. Films during the period could adopt the stock generic pattern or discard previously held essentials of the romantic comedy. Of all the 1970s films, *Annie Hall* seems to have been both visually the most influential, and narratively the most unrepeatable: a work of conscious iconoclasm, it breaks with many generic conventions, most notably the happy ending. *Annie Hall* was not the first film of this period, however, to jettison the usual elements of the romantic comedy. While innovative, it has a clear predecessor in a film such as *Harold and Maude* (1971) and in fact inherits tendencies observable in a different strand of satirical American comedy evolving in the late 1960s, exemplified in *The Graduate* (1967).

The radical romantic comedy is often willing to abandon the emphasis on making sure the couple ends up together, regardless of likelihood, instead striving to interrogate the ideology of romance. Brian Henderson (1978) sees the films of this period realising that the romantic comedy genre has been killed because of the changes in society. He traces the uneasy development of the genre against a background of male-oriented buddy movies, paranoiac films and ultra-violence, deciding that the de-emphasising of the female's role sounds the death knell of romantic comedy: 'There can be no romantic comedy without strong heroines' (1978:18). Henderson does not conclude, as I have suggested in the previous chapter, that this downgrading of the female character arose once her *raison d'être* – saying no to the wrong kind of sex – was removed by the pill, and thus that changing societal attitudes to sex were responsible for this shift in the romantic comedy's terrain.

Henderson does, however, feel that the question overtly phrased in Michael Ritchie's film *Semi-Tough* (1977), 'How come we never fucked?', is tacitly raised in all romantic comedies but must never be uttered (1978: 21). The evolutions in cinema which made it possible, in the 1970s, for characters not only to provide the answer but to ask the question aloud, he asserts, imperilled the romantic comedy as it had been for forty years. With barriers to consummation removed by changes in both birth control and social mores, what was there to stop the romantic comedy heroine from sleeping with the hero? Henderson posits that without such barriers romantic comedy loses its point. While sex was postponed, the couple had to engage in verbal foreplay which substituted for, forecast and enticed the other towards, the eventual act. Without its postponement, sex was all there was, so goodbye verbal foreplay and hence, Henderson feels, good-bye romance. Changing social structures thus impacted directly on the romantic comedy's ideologies and narratives. This fostered an evolution of the genre which, suddenly aware of the possible obsolescence of its pre-occupations, determined to examine, self-consciously, these preoccupations and their traditional conventions.

Contexts of the radical romantic comedy

Just as the screwball and the sex comedy were products of their particular originating times, the romantic comedies of the 1970s also reflected contemporary preoccupations and anxieties; it is important to note that the radicalism of many of these texts, however, was absorbed from the political and social upheavals of the late 1960s. Those factors which affected the romantic comedy and altered it so drastically were not only the skirmishes attendant on the evolution of the feminist, black and gay rights movements, but a number of other events of great social and political consequence. The single year of 1968, for example, saw incidents – as diverse as they were influential – which included the assassinations of black activist Dr Martin Luther King and presidential candidate Robert Kennedy; the Miss America protests where the ritualised actions of several female activists coined the term 'bra burners' for an entire generation of 'women's libbers'; the publication of Virginia Masters and William Johnson's book, *Human Sexual Response*, which underlined Kinsey's findings in the previous decade about the importance of the sexual experience for women; the final abandonment of the Production Code and its replacement by a ratings system; and the high-profile massacre of innocent Vietnamese civilians by US soldiers at My Lai. Violence and change seemed, at the end of the 1960s, to be all-pervasive: old certainties were swept away, old assumptions extinguished.

The romantic comedies of the early to mid-1970s clearly reflect this mood of upheaval in their willingness to jettison former rules. Ironically, however, even as movie theatres were showing films which tapped into the energy and potential for national change which had inspired the previous decade, people began moving away from intellectual involvement with contemporary events towards a less engaged point-of-view. Political fervour and social optimism seemed to belong to the 1960s; the 1970s enshrined cynical apathy. Coupled with this move away from big issues and political movements was a corresponding turning inwards; social commentators registered this developing introspection, dubbing the 1970s 'the Me decade' (Wolfe 1976: 162). Many of the romantic comedies of the later 1970s reflect this new spirit of self-absorption: *Starting Over* (1979), for example, alludes to women's self-defence classes, sex manuals, notions about the 'right and wrong kinds of orgasm', post-divorce support groups, self-help literature and even self-help songs. Jessica (Candice Bergen) is satirised effectively from the very opening of the film by the rampant narcissism observable in her songs, especially since delivered in a stridently off-key voice. These songs, such as 'Easy For You' and 'Better Than Ever', are parodies but close to the spirit of such contemporary hits as Candi Staton's 'Young Hearts Run Free' which, containing lines such as 'my mind must be free to learn all I can about me' and 'self-preservation is what's really going on today', clearly taps into the 1970s culture of self-absorption.

A new era of greater realism in the depiction of sex and violence began after the end of the Production Code and its replacement by a ratings system. At the same time as greater frankness in the depiction of screen sex was permissible, contemporary headlines underscored the need for greater realism in facing the challenges of modern relationships: the percentage of marriages ending in divorce rocketed, statistics revealed that there were more single women than single men inhabiting the big American cities, abortion became a publicly-debated issue on an unprecedented scale with the historic Roe vs. Wade case of 1973. The world of sex, love and romance seemed a very different place from that of even a decade previously; given the large number of these factors, we might expect to be seeing films emerging at this time which centred on the inevitability of couples breaking up, or devoted to exploring life as a single woman or man, or to find an abundance of divorce comedies. While many of the romantic comedies of the 1970s *do* include these ingredients, as romantic comedies they often end in the traditional way with the formation of a heterosexual couple. *Starting Over*, for example, begins by acknowledging that contemporary life includes the possibility of marriage ending in divorce, but then ignores this realist tendency by having the hero establish a new relationship and, as in the sex comedy, ushering in the end of the film just as the new couple have overcome all obstacles to being together. While the frank acceptance of pre-marital sexual relations marks this and similar films as being from a post-pill era, texts such as *Starting Over* continue the convention of ending without exploring the factors ranged against the happy ever after.

Romantic comedies from the 1970s can also be seen to have been affected by some late 1960s films which took up the sex comedies' accent on female/male relations but in a more politically engaged, satirical way. *The Graduate*, for example, does not seem to be a full romantic comedy because, although the hero, Benjamin Braddock (Dustin Hoffman), does fall in love with a girl, Elaine (Katharine Ross), the story is more about his inability to fit into society than about her importance to his life. In the famous ending, in what seems a self-conscious rebuttal of *It Happened One Night*, Benjamin arrives at Elaine's wedding to another man. While the 1934 text averts potential disaster by having Ellie run away just before taking her vows, *The Graduate* signals its awareness of harsher realities: the marriage has been completed. But then Elaine joins Benjamin and the couple flee, ending up on a bus together as their pursuers recede into the background. While *The Graduate* thus presents a romantic story, it is interested in upsetting the conventions of this genre rather than upholding them.

Figure 9: What comes after the 'happy ever after' in *The Graduate*?

Benjamin has previously had an affair with Elaine's mother, Mrs Robinson (Anne Bancroft): the narrative arc of the film thus subverts the usual boy meets girl convention, replacing it with boy meets woman, gets woman, ditches woman for her daughter, loses daughter, gets daughter. Unlike the standard romantic comedy, however, which asserts that in winning his true love the hero will have the one thing he needs for future happiness, *The Graduate*'s final moments imply that the impulsive elopement may have been just one more mistake. This undercutting of familiar conclusions establishes *The Graduate* as detached from, and critical of, the more traditional ending where the achievement of the final reel coupling is all that is necessary. Ben and Elaine's silence on the bus suggests there will be life after the happy ever after, but it may involve the couple splitting up.

Sexual desire and pleasure, as important for both genders, is accented in these films. While many of the 1970s films, such as *Starting Over*, *The Heartbreak Kid* (1972) and *10* (1979) seem driven, like *The Graduate* in the late 1960s, by the male protagonist's sexual obsessions, other films from the decade illustrate the new awareness and acceptance of sexual desire in women. *On a Clear Day You Can See Forever* (1970) and *An Unmarried Woman* (1978) bracket the decade, both insisting narratively and visually on the importance of sexual fulfilment within women's lives. The former film, a vehicle for Barbra Streisand, adapted from a 1965 musical, allows the star to showcase both voice and acting talents by performing two roles: kooky Jewish New York psychic Daisy Gamble and her previous incarnation, a nineteenth-century Englishwoman, Melinda. While Daisy strives to become the perfect wife to her boring fiancé, flashbacks indicate how Melinda triumphantly ignored the dictates of society about appropriate female behaviour and desires. The scene in which Melinda attempts to seduce a young man clearly demonstrates that, post-Production Code, film as a medium was able to tap into the new societal acceptance of physical desire in women: at a banquet Melinda stares boldly at her prey across the table, suggestively stroking and fondling her wine glass with her hands and mouth.

An Unmarried Woman continues this exploration of female sexuality, looking at the problems facing the large demographic of single women in New York City in search of 'a decent guy'. Erica Benton (Jill Clayburgh) appears to have one, her husband, Martin (Michael Murphy); congratulating herself on her good fortune after meeting her three female friends who are either miserably married, bitterly divorced or frantically dating, she tells him 'I'd hate to join the crowd', the mass of women in the city looking for love. But she is about to join it: her husband reveals that he has been having an affair, and is leaving her for the other woman. The film then explores Erica's options as she moves through rage, depression, therapy, and tentatively into sexual experimentation, as she has sex with other men after 17 years with her husband. Interestingly, when Saul (Alan Bates), the man with whom she will form the new couple by the end of the film, is introduced to her, the next scene finds them after their first sex together, with her preparing to leave and he seeking some kind of emotional reassurance. There is no big build up to their first coupling, nor even a significant amount of dialogue between the two to suggest an attraction. Saul's introduction in this way then works to strengthen Erica's own surprise when he turns out to become a longer-term prospect. Although the film ends with him driving away from her, leaving her in the midst of bustling New York with an over-sized painting to manoeuvre across town, the viewer has no doubt either that she is equal to the task or that he will return to her. An Unmarried Woman uses the character of Erica, but also her girlfriends, acquaintances, female therapist and daughter to explore the importance of sex to women. The women regularly share information about the number and derivation of orgasms, the technique of their lovers, their own solutions to the shortage of eligible men. Erica's therapist seems to have taken a female lover; Erica's own answer, for a time, is not to seek anything more than casual sex. Because this is a romantic comedy, however, she eventually finds the one man whose artistic, sensual and witty character exactly complements hers.

The radical romantic comedy produced in the 1970s, then, was clearly influenced by the political upheavals of the end of the previous decade, and reveals, at least at the beginning of the period, an engagement with the potential for rejecting established conventions, of both text and society. As the decade wore on, however, and political fervour seemed now naïve, contemporary films began to note a new self-absorption in their protagonists which echoed the self-awareness the films themselves were experiencing.

Characteristics of radical romantic comedy

While films within both screwball and sex comedy sub-genres shared thematic and visual elements, it has been argued that the 1970s romantic comedy is so different from earlier models that it represents a complete break from them. Close investigation of films from this period, however, reveals that the texts display sufficient common tendencies to represent another evolution of the genre. It is true that, perhaps for the first time in Hollywood history, romantic comedies were fewer in number than before, *Variety* hailing both *What's Up, Doc?* ('Murf' 1972) and *Annie Hall* ('Mack' 1977) as rarities. Although less numerous, the radical romantic comedy still existed as a discrete form with specific preoccupations.

Several of the key characteristics of the romantic comedy films from this period are generated by the conscious breaking of conventions from the earlier sub-genres. Whereas both screwball and sex comedy made use of ideas of disguise and masquerade, and inversions of the norm, the radical romantic comedies choose to inflect these more literally, Erica's life being inverted when she goes from being a wife to a newly-single woman. However, when a character does make use of masquerade, it is generally the male, as in the sex comedy, but the radical romantic comedy withholds the exploding of the scheming male's plot which was such a necessary part of the sex comedy's narrative structure and humour. By withholding the revelation of the man's deceit, the radical romantic comedy can be seen as suggesting both that everyone lives a lie, and that the liar, in the end, is the one who suffers most. In *The Heartbreak Kid*, for example, the hero Lenny (Charles Brodin) is first encountered in a montage sequence getting to know a woman he meets in a bar; the first sustained scene is of their marriage. On their honeymoon, Lenny begins to realise he knows little about Lila (Jeannie Berlin) and likes what he discovers even less. When she is confined to bed with sunburn he meets another young woman – richer, more beautiful, but also spoiled and manipulative. This new woman, Kelly (Cybill Shepherd), seems to set her cap at Lenny, necessitating that he lie to his new wife about his absences. As his lies escalate and his stories become more fantastic, the viewer waits for the moment when he will be caught out: he can almost be forgiven in advance, so enormous will the come-down be when he is apprehended. But there is no explosion: Lenny manages to extricate himself from his five-day marriage without admitting he has found a better partner. While the film permits Lenny to 'win' Kelly, the narrative ending with *their* wedding, elements of the music, *mise-en-scène* and dialogue work to confirm that the new marriage will be as empty as the one he scrambled to leave. The same tune, the Carpenters' 'Close To You', is played at both receptions, underlining the actual distance between Lenny and either of the brides; the final shot is of the groom sitting alone inanely humming the tune and looking, while a little dazed, still optimistic. This conclusion brings the film to a halt at the traditional point, with a wedding, but can be seen here to be using this to suggest that there will be little else to celebrate in the relationship. The film refuses to go on into the future with Lenny because while he lives in a fantasy world, dreaming of finding the perfect woman, he has no future. Lenny's deceit rebounds on him because it blinds him to the reality of his relationship with the manipulative Kelly, upon whose reasons for desiring the marriage the film does not even begin to speculate. Lenny's optimism shows him to be naïve about the woman he has struggled to win: he refuses to ask why Kelly should choose him when she is clearly inundated with other, more appropriate, offers. His narcissism is also apparent in the matched scenes where he has sex with Lila and with Kelly. In the first Lila demands to be told during sex that it is wonderful, to Lenny's obvious annoyance; in the second, he fervently repeats the same sorts of phrases – 'I knew it could be like this!' – unaware that Kelly is looking bored. Lenny's naivety means he ignores, or is unconscious of the importance of, parity in sexual relations: the radical romantic comedy indicates that healthy relationships provide sexual satisfaction for women too. Lenny's ultimate crime is to have a 1960s sense of potential in a 1970s world, while failing to recognise both that his optimism and belief in the possibility of change have become anachronisms, and that the new decade demands introspection. Lenny is outmoded because he believes he can change his life by changing his wife, rather than by looking inside himself.

This emphasis on the self carries across from the characters in the texts of this period to become the central trope of those texts. The major thematic concerns of the radical romantic comedy all derive from issues of self-reflexivity, a heightened consciousness of self which these films exhibit across three main areas:

- self-reflexivity about the *romantic relationship* and the importance of sex to both genders
- self-reflexivity *as a film text* in a tradition of other film texts
- self-reflexivity as a *modern and more realistic form of romantic comedy* in contrast to earlier texts

The radical romantic comedy acknowledges that its characters are in search of meaningful and satisfying relationships; and, sometimes to the contrary, that they also seek romance. The idea that romance and satisfaction could be opposite values is new to these films, as the characters struggle to be realistic and up-to-date whilst still yearning for the type of instant attraction and eternal devotion assumed to be possible by older texts. In *The Goodbye Girl* (1977), the central female character, Paula (Marsha Mason), is a divorcée with a daughter; as the film begins she finds a note from her latest lover telling her their relationship is over. Worse still, he has sub-let the apartment she and her daughter live in: Elliot (Richard Dreyfuss) the new tenant, arrives in the middle of a rainstorm and refuses to leave. While the pair act out the motions of hating each other at first sight, which might incline the viewer to assume they will thus naturally become a couple, the film shows Paula resisting Elliot's charms, despite an attraction to him, because she is afraid of being hurt again. The couple talk about the changing status of their relationship, testing each others' and their own feelings: Elliot asks 'Do you get the feeling something is happening between us?' He then proceeds to woo Paula by inviting her for dinner, staging this event overtly as a romantic gesture. He leaves a trail of clues for her to find him on the roof of their apartment building; he has lights strung overhead, candles, music, is wearing a white tuxedo and hat, and greets her with a Humphrey Bogart impression, seemingly to evoke that actor's persona in the romantic classic *Casablanca* (1942). Elliot's Bogart impression gestures back to an older, less self-conscious, form of romantic cinema, permitting him to express his feelings through drawing on conventions they both understand. He also sings her the song 'How About You?', a Freed and Lane classic which hints, in its lyrics, at the anxious search everyone undergoes for someone with similar interests ('I like New York in June, how about you?/I like a Gershwin tune, how about you?'), as well as at the banality of those interests until shared with a loved one. The song was made famous by its performance by Judy Garland and Mickey Rooney in *Babes on Broadway* (1941) although it has appeared in other films. Again, however, by evoking a past moment when romance seemed easier, Elliot expresses awareness of the different times he and Paula inhabit but also indicates he will try to show emotion and commitment the old-fashioned way. By having Elliot himself singing the words to Paula, as they slowly dance on the roof, the film indicates his willingness to try at romance. While more recent films use romantic musical classics played extra-diegetically to suggest the emotional attraction of couples, *The Goodbye Girl* lets Elliot perform his own song to confirm his greater commitment to the possibility of true love, even if they are both aware of the likely failures, even if the trappings of romance need to be evoked by borrowings from earlier texts (*Casablanca* and Mickey/Judy movies), and even if Elliot's efforts seem to be mocked by the weather, as the skies open and his elaborate evening is rained upon.

Elliot's gestures are recognised by Paula as signalling he too desires something it would seem naïve to want: an old-fashioned love affair. She acknowledges his efforts and their success at impressing her when she admits 'I'm a sucker for romance'. Paula is used to being short-changed in relationships and struggles against what Elliot is offering because it seems too good to be true. Because the film is a romantic comedy, it ends by assuring that Elliot really does love Paula: but because it is a radical romantic comedy, it also ends with the lovers apart. As yet another rainstorm lashes New York, Elliot goes off to the airport, leaving his guitar behind as proof of his intentions to return. Ending with Elliot's exit in a cab, while Paula waves goodbye, gives the film's conclusion an energy, a sense of not being the end, which seems to contradict the pain both lovers will feel at the other's absence, and seems much more upbeat, despite their actual parting, than the ending of *The Heartbreak Kid* where the couple are physically together but emotionally distant.

In looking back to older films for clues on how to make romantic love visible, Elliot implies that times have changed and emotions cannot be expressed so unself-consciously now, a theme echoed by other radical romantic comedies which show that self-reflexivity about romance was not just confined to film characters but extends to contemporary texts themselves, overtly acknowledging themselves as films within various traditions. *What's Up, Doc?*'s reworking of *Bringing Up Baby*, for example, clearly evinces this self-referentiality: the actors, especially Streisand, seem aware of themselves as characters in a film and highlight this by direct looks to camera and quotations from other screen texts. Underlining the film's title, Streisand – eating a carrot – invokes the anarchic force of Bugs Bunny in her opening remark to O'Neal, 'What's up, Doc?' She later quotes Rick's line, 'Of all the gin joints in all the towns in all the world...' from *Casablanca*, drawing attention again to this classic romantic text, as well as reciting back to O'Neal the most famous line from his own recent hit, *Love Story* (1970): 'Love means never having to say you're sorry.' The film thus acknowledges its own status as film, as love story and as slapstick comedy in the mould of cartoons and screwball, inviting viewers to recognise lines and situations, draw analogies with earlier texts and enjoy its manipulation of their elements. This awareness that audiences would share the recognition of older conventions and take pleasure in their re-use infuses many of the films of this period.

The third form that the self-referentiality of these texts takes is awareness of themselves as modern films, having to juggle the opposing claims of realism and romanticism. As romantic comedies, they want to bring about the happy union of a woman and a man; as modern films, they have to show themselves to be beyond the naivety that such uncomplicated couplings rely on. This results in a group of films which displays its realism very openly, but can sometimes seem ashamed of endings which keep the couple together. In such films the modern elements – topical references to women's liberation, birth control, psychoanalysis, as well as more frank sexual language and swearing – can seem like trappings draped uneasily over an older framework to give it a superficial trendiness. As mentioned, *Starting Over* is one such text, layering on the details of contemporary urban living for realistic purposes to distract the viewer from the conservatism of the basic plot, which retains the traditional boy meets, loses and re-gets girl armature.

The radical romantic comedies are aware of film history and genre conventions, and are frequently happy to jettison many of the elements of earlier forms. For example, texts are more prepared to end openly, with a decision yet to be made, reminiscent of the influential final moments of François Truffaut's *Les Quatre Cents Coups* (*The 400 Blows*, 1959), where the camera just freezes the image of Antoine Doinel (Jean-Paul Léaud) as he runs along a beach, not indicating a purpose, just showing his intent to keep moving and then, ironically, denying this motion by freezing it. Besides employing endings which evoked the openness of European art cinema, rather than the conventional Hollywood conclusion which saw all story strands nicely tied up, the radical romantic comedy was also prepared to end unhappily. *Harold and Maude*, a film which the revolted *Variety* sarcastically claimed had 'all the charm and gaiety of a burning orphanage', not only paired a 20-year old boy with an about-to-be-80-year-old woman, but allowed their *consummated* relationship to end with her suicide. While sadness does accrue to the end of the film, at the last there is an upbeat moment when, having sent his car crashing off a cliff, Harold (Bud Cort) is discovered not to be inside it. Having learned from Maude (Ruth Gordon) to love life, he skips away playing a guitar and singing the song she taught him.

While it is possible to say with certainty, therefore, that the romantic comedy before the 1970s was about love and romance, and would end happily with the couple's union, the radical romantic comedy, for a short period, was interested to see what became of the genre if more realistic elements were permitted space. Loss and death were allowed into the stories alongside love and marriage, and the traditional happy ending of the romantic comedy in these films might be subverted, conclusions occurring without the central union assured or even with it prevented by death or failure. This acceptance of more realistic elements in the films' narratives was matched by more realistic language, with a marked increase in swearing and discussion of sexual matters. There is a very noticeable emphasis on the importance of sexual satisfaction to women, as well as to men, and the acknowledgement of female sexual desire. In *The Goodbye Girl*, for example, Paula propositions Elliot at the end of their romantic dinner, showing that while she is 'a sucker for romance', she also desires a sexual relationship. The newness of this awareness of an active female sexuality can be seen in Elliot's surprise at her frankness:

Paula: Are we going to sleep with each other tonight?
Elliot: (laughs) You know, of all the right upfront girls I know, you are the right upfrontest! ... Well, how do you feel about it?
Paula: Nervous. A pushover, but nervous.

Paula admits she wants sex with Elliot, and is mature enough to confirm both that she is anxious and that this will not prevent her from going to bed with him. *The Goodbye Girl* shows the tendency towards realism observable in the radical romantic comedy by overtly admitting that Paula has had previous lovers, and not condemning her for this, but allowing her the opportunity to try again for true love. The texts which make up the radical romantic comedy sub-genre are aware of the almost inevitable failure of romantic love and allow their characters to strive for it nonetheless.

In addition to these three differently-inflected uses of self-awareness, the radical romantic comedies share several more micro-tropes also. Most noticeably, they are very urban and, while it seems now a cliché that every romantic comedy should be set in New York City, at the time that these texts emerged it was more common to condemn the city as a place of danger than to see it as the Edenic setting of romance. The typical view of the metropolis was one in which it fostered the moral sickness commented on by, and embodied in, Travis Bickle (Robert De Niro), in *Taxi Driver* (1976); 1970s audiences were thus being treated to a novelty in the contemporary suggestion that the city could be capable of fostering an intimate couple, rather than just a morass of alienated strangers. The emphasis on the urban extends to the fact that many scenes are filmed on the city streets, or seemingly in real apartments, rather than the luxury sets common to both the screwball and the sex comedy. Characters stroll around identifiable locations in the radical romantic comedy, underlining its sense of realism, rather than inhabiting a city made up of matte shots and elaborate nightclub, restaurant and hotel sets, as in the older sub-genres. Costumes, too, are much more realistic, outfits being worn which reflect the buying potential and tastes of the characters rather than the total vision of a designer.

One final mini-trope to note in these radical romantic comedies is the music. These 1970s films frequently use romantic classics from the 1940s and earlier in an attempt to recapture something of the sense of romance from a time before the gloss and glibness of the sex comedy brought an archness to proceedings. As noted, *The Goodbye Girl* employs the 1941 favourite 'How About You?', and allows its central male character, Elliot, to sing the lyrics himself, rather than just playing a pre-recorded version of the love song. This emphasis on authentic involvement, even if accompanied by embarrassment, rather than the utilisation of a pre-packaged song to evoke a pre-packaged emotion, is what often separates the use of romantic classics in these 1970s texts from their employment in films a decade later. While the radical romantic comedy, in using such songs, can be seen indulging in nostalgia, this is informed by a yearning for a past when romance seemed less doomed to fail, and people could therefore (it was assumed) go about proclaiming their feelings without such complex clusters of emotions. Such films from the 1970s use nostalgia consciously to comment on their awareness of changed circumstances, the contemporary distance from former romantic securities. Increasingly, however, as the 1980s shaded into the 1990s, later texts began to rely on musical cues to evoke emotions in the viewer, so that instead of trying to create moods through narrative, dialogue and character, they simply employed well-known music to conjure the necessary resonances. Unlike these more cynical texts of the following decades, the radical romantic comedies are self-aware of their own textual existence but manage to find something heroic about continuing to battle for true love against the odds. They are aware of the obsolescence of their own genre, and this produces the self-consciousness observable in such texts: they do not use self-referentiality as an opportunity to disavow what they are doing.

Having drawn together a list of characteristics common to this period's romantic comedies, it becomes possible to offer a working definition of this grouping:

The radical romantic comedy generally retains the basic framework (boy meets, loses, regains girl) of the standard romantic comedy, but makes much of its own realism in certain areas – language, sexual frankness – being prepared to discard older conventions and frequently permitting a much more open ending.

Annie Hall will now be considered as a prime example of the radical romantic comedy. As will be seen, in ending by insisting on the dissolution of the couple, this film goes beyond the radicalism of other contemporary texts which might leave matters open at the conclusion but did not often risk evoking the negative emotions resulting from a definite unhappy ending.

Radical romantic comedy case study: Annie Hall

Annie Hall, following the particular conventions of its time, uses the established framework of the genre but supplements it with its own increased realism in the portrayal of the romance and its breakdown. This realism is not restricted to the trappings of 1970s urban life – cocaine parties, nightclubs, literary and political allusions – but extends to the film's treatment of sex as an important, indeed defining, part of individuality. Supremely, *Annie Hall* demonstrates the ultimate form of two of the contemporary genre's particular concerns: self-referentiality and radicalism.

Woody Allen's film acknowledges its self-awareness in the three areas outlined above, demonstrating self-reflexivity about contemporary romance, about film texts, and about the romantic comedy film specifically. Skillfully, it does these things with a light touch, hoping to coax the audience to laughter and self-recognition rather than feeling intimidated by its cleverness. Above all it is marked by an appearance of simplicity which serves to mask the actual complexity of its timeframe and structure.

Annie Hall confronts the realities of romance and sex from its very first scene: Alvy (Woody Allen) talks to the camera directly, as if it were both a true-life confession and one of his stand-up comedy performances. Seeming to ramble aimlessly, he is really trying to come to terms with the latest evolution of his romantic life, as he eventually admits:

> Annie and I broke up and I still can't get my mind around that, you know, I keep sifting the pieces of the relationship through my mind and examining my life and trying to figure out where did the screw up come, you know? A year ago, we were ... in love...

The whole of the film's narrative can be understood as Alvy's attempt to sift 'the pieces of the relationship', working out where things went wrong through examining his life, trying to explain his actions. The narrative becomes a therapeutic activity for Alvy, the seemingly random delving into his past a patient's work during a psychoanalytic session. Being in therapy is a common activity for many of Allen's characters, and in *Annie Hall* he redoubles the emphasis on 'the talking cure' by foregrounding references to analysis, as well as allowing Alvy's reminiscences to act as a 98-minute therapy session. The film further taps into the zeitgeist through its insistence on the pitfalls of romantic love, sexual attraction and marriage. Unlike earlier films, such as the sex comedy, which chose to believe in the possible transformation of the playboy rake into the monogamous husband, the 1970s radical romantic comedy shows itself to be aware of the difficulties of modern love. The film notes that sexual attraction fades, people have serial romances, Alvy himself has two failed marriages, Annie (Diane Keaton) loses interest in sex and cannot relax without taking marijuana, puts Alvy off or, giving in, endures the act by detaching her attention. The film's bravery in confronting the realities of modern love culminates in its ending which insists that the couple, though meeting again and enjoying each other's company, does not ultimately re-form. Within the film's three-fold exploration of self-reflexivity, this ending is as resolutely appropriate to the realistic portrayal of modern love, and to the film's acknowledgement of itself as a film text within certain traditions, as it is in conscious opposition to the usual generic ending. The self-referential nature of the text is there-fore crucial to its narrative structure, all three forms of self-awareness directing the story towards an open, unresolved ending rather than a neatly-finished form of closure.

It is perhaps in its self-reflexivity as a film text within various film traditions that *Annie Hall* is most dazzling, the film consciously employing various filmic techniques, in addition to the usual 'invisible' style of Hollywood filmmaking. Through this self-conscious experimentation with technique the film marks itself as inspired as much by European art films as by Hollywood cinema. David Bordwell (1979) suggests such films share conventions which represent their conscious structuring of an opposition to classic cinema. These include an abandonment of a clear cause and effect narrative, using a more episodic structure, showing interest in ideas rather than entertainment, and an obsession with sexuality, blurring fantasy and reality, and leaving an ambiguous or open-ended conclusion, all via a medium which can momentarily reject the standard rules, so that montage, jump cuts and long takes appear frequently. These characteristics, present within *Annie Hall*, indicate the film positioning itself within a European art cinema tradition, especially in its complicated timeframe, which recounts different moments of the couple's affair without using a straightforward chronology or signposts to indicate movements in time.

Annie Hall's use of filmic devices designed to show off its self-aware-ness begins right at the film's opening when Alvy speaks direct to camera in the stand-up routine confessional mentioned above. Because of Allen's then-accepted status as a comedian, the transgressive nature of this direct look can be momentarily minimised. However, when during Alvy's fre-quently enacted memories of the past – which themselves act as homages to the work of Ingmar Bergman – he looks at the camera, the device is more noticeable, as when his first wife Allison (Carole Kane) accuses him of using the Kennedy assassination as an excuse not to have sex with her, and Alvy turns to the camera, exclaiming, 'Oh my God! She's right!' The film is both aware of the artificiality of the scene – it is being staged as a memory in a film – and playing with the usual rule of filmmaking which decrees the per-former not break the illusion of the narrative by acknowledging the camera or the viewer its presence implies. Another of the devices used to underline most directly the debt Allen feels to European art cinema, sub-titling, is wittily employed in the scene where Annie and Alvy first start tentatively flirting. The film suggests the intellectual conversation the pair are having is a foreign language to the characters themselves, as the 'translation' appearing underneath the frame reveals their real anxieties and desires: 'I wonder what she looks like naked'; 'I bet he thinks I'm a yo-yo.' While suggesting that the pair are internally split, saying one thing but thinking something quite different, the film cements the two as a couple by showing them *both* similarly divided. This parity tends to operate across the whole film, as when both are permitted internal monologues which the audience can hear. In one instance, however, the device is not employed equally, although its use does revolve around yet another technique which Allen wittily uses to demonstrate his awareness of filmmaking methods. This is the two instances of the use of split-screen: in both cases, the split is not equal, devoting half of the frame to each character, but instead allotting a third of the screen to Annie and the larger portion to Alvy. The first use of this is at the disastrous lunch with Annie's parents (Colleen Dewhurst and Donald Symington). On the second, even more pointed occasion, both characters are seeing their therapists. Through the *mise-en-scène* of each part of the screen the film provides information about the type of analysis each character is experiencing and, by extension, gives further insights into their personalities. Annie's female analyst (Veronica Radburn), unseen, has an office marked by modernist furniture, with an abstract painting on the white wall and an upright chair for Annie to sit in. Alvy's male analyst (Humphrey Davis) by contrast features as part of the *mise-en-scène* himself: a much more traditional figure, be-suited, with a moustache and his hands pensively steepled in front of him, Alvy's analyst fits in with the surroundings of big leather chairs, a couch for Alvy to recline on, Egyptian artefacts. These basic oppositions – modern/traditional, female/male, and, significantly, seemingly helpful/static – go some way to redress the imbalance of power in Annie's favour. While Alvy may be seen to concentrate on his own view of the story, to privilege it against Annie's, director Allen allows *mise-en-scène* and the unequal split-screen to comment on the male character's self-obsession. Simultaneously, the repetition of dialogue across the two analytical sessions reinforces the couple's similarities ('How often do you have sex?'/'Do you often make love?') at the same time as their differences ('All the time, maybe three times a week'/'Hardly ever, maybe three times a week').

Figure 10: Split-screen and *mise-en-scène* used to contrast analytical styles in *Annie Hall*

Figure 11: Alvy's Wicked Queen

In addition to constant verbal references to other films and directors, *Annie Hall* provides visual references too, incorporating two clips from *The Sorrow and the Pity* (1974) and also providing a cartoon version of the hero enamoured of a Wicked Queen like the one in Disney's *Snow White and the Seven Dwarfs* (1939). The final technique employed is montage, where a succession of images shown at the end of the film reference various moments of the affair. This montage will be dealt with in more detail below, in discussing the film's conclusion.

The final type of self-referentiality is the film's awareness of itself as a romantic comedy both within and against a tradition of such films. This manifests itself in the ambivalence revealed towards romantic love through the film's insistence on the realistic treatment of sexuality, but also using two songs to evoke more conventional treatments of romance. Amongst the details of contemporary sexual life there are sex scenes where one or both characters ends frustrated, references to oral sex and masturbation, and, typically of the texts of this time, an emphasis on the importance of sexual choice for women, whether this be Allison demanding sex or Annie avoiding it. When Annie sings the two romantic classics ('It Had To Be You' by Kahn and Jones, 1924, and 'Seems Like Old Times', by Loeb and Lombardo, 1946) she is referencing older versions of the romantic myth, in direct contrast to the contemporary approach taken by the film. The film thus acknowledges the seductive pull of this traditional view of romance, admitting its allure even while using Annie's rather artful performance of the songs to establish them as performed moments, rather than ones of authenticity for the character.

Annie Hall allows itself a final comment on traditional romantic narratives through the medium of Alvy's play. The film has just shown Alvy and Annie meeting in California but failing to resolve their differences, and parting. In the play rehearsal two young actors, physically reminiscent of Alvy and Annie, repeat the characters' conversation, but with the significant difference that Sally capitulates: 'Wait. I'm going to go with you. I love you.' Acknowledging the hackneyed effect of this, Alvy speaks again direct to camera in his defence: 'Well, what do you want? It was my first play...' By introducing this potential happy ending but allowing the clichéd dialogue and consciously 'bad' performance of the young actors to reveal its artificiality, the film prepares the viewer for an ending which will maintain emotional truth by sacrificing the lovers' reunion.

Annie Hall's conclusion maintains the film's self-reflexive tendencies: it overtly owes much to European cinema; as a modern text about love it feels it must end without the usual reconciliation, especially as this establishes it against the traditions of romantic comedy. The ending is also extremely skillful in seeming to unroll naturally, when actually it is a highly complex structure, with opposing sound and visual tracks. An examination of how this ending is constructed and what this construction achieves indicates the true radicalism of the text.

Alvy reports that he met Annie again, back in New York City. The scene presents a dense structure of voice and image: we hear Annie singing 'Seems Like Old Times' again as Alvy comments on their encounter and we see the pair talking animatedly at lunch. Then 18 shots of scenes from the couple's relationship unfold, without a linear chronology, in a montage accompanied only by Annie's singing. As the montage comes to an end, Alvy's voice resumes the narration and the camera maintains its distance from the pair as they say goodbye. Before, they had been inside a restaurant, and the camera outside, regarding them through the glass: now the positions are reversed, but the camera is permitted no nearer and the viewer cannot hear what the pair are saying, but listens instead to Annie singing and Alvy's voice over hers narrating the events. Alvy's final speech demonstrates that he realises he was lucky to have known Annie and that though their

Figure 12: The final empty frames of the film

romance will not continue, the memories of the good times can sustain him as he waits for the next love affair to begin. This acknowledgement of seriality is very much at odds with the usual romantic ending but helps to evade the downbeat quality the ending would have had if marked by Alvy's realisation, too late, that Annie was the only love of his life. Alvy's final lines are spoken after he has watched Annie leave, and then too has departed. Significantly, the film frame stays empty for some seconds, creating a mood of longing and suggesting that either of the pair might return. However, the film ends without further action, Alvy falling silent just before Annie sings the final word of her song. The frame's emptiness especially recalls the conclusion of Antonioni's *L'Eclisse* (*The Eclipse*, 1962), in which two lovers, having agreed to meet at a certain corner, both stand each other up. Only the camera attends the rendezvous, waiting fruitlessly for seven minutes for someone to arrive. Allen softens (and shortens) this downbeat ending slightly by having both members of the couple indicated even in the empty scene: while physically absent the former lovers are both equally present through their voices.

Evolution of the radical romantic comedy

If the films of the subsequent decades inherit the visual tropes but ignore the thematic ones of the radical romantic comedy, where are the films that do pick up on this sub-genre's openness, its willingness to risk an unhappy or at least untidy ending? It is possible to see the influence of these texts persisting into later years, despite the almost total hegemony of the neo-traditional romantic comedy, as will be discussed shortly. Interestingly, the films which are prepared to maintain the radical romantic comedy's emphasis on balancing the competing claims of realism and romance tend to be the ones also exploring the one taboo which even the 1970s texts would not attempt. While *Harold and Maude* courted box office and critical disaster by insisting that a bright but immature 20-year-old boy could find emotional and sexual fulfilment with an octogenarian, it at least maintained the heterosexuality of its central couple. It seems that the final convention of the romantic comedy to be disposed of is the gender of the protagonists. To date there has yet to be a successful mainstream romantic comedy which permits the narrative to focus on a homosexual couple, although there have been several financially profitable independent films which have done so, such as *Go Fish* (1994), *Jeffrey* (1995) and *Kissing Jessica Stein* (2001).

While such films manifest an awareness of the potential pitfalls of modern romance, dating, sex and relationships, a commitment to more realistic, non-sugary endings *and* to showing homosexual love can cause problems. This is perhaps one reason, apart from the obvious conservatism of the main studios, why the precedent offered by these independent productions has yet to be followed by a mainstream film. These independent romantic comedies treating gay and lesbian relationships are maintaining that everyone becomes an irrational fool once in love. Establishing the homosexual couple thus provides the same material for comic misunderstandings as a heterosexual pairing. However, by joining the sexual skirmishes and romantic longings of a gay couple with a downbeat ending, films may appear to suggest that a homosexual love affair is doomed to fail. Ironically, the very films that work to show that gays and lesbians are subject to the same longings for romantic love and sexual fulfilment as heterosexuals would thus reinforce a subtext of inevitable failure for such relationships. *Kissing Jessica Stein* shows Jessica (Jennifer Westfeldt) on a series of disastrous first dates with men, establishing her as bright but brittle and neurotic, yearning for love but too frightened of rejection to be approachable. Seeing a personal ad which quotes her favourite poet, Jessica thinks this must be fate until she realises the ad is by a woman; desperate, she calls her anyway and they then begin a slow courtship. Helen (Heather

Juergensen) is experimenting with dating women also, having chosen to explore this side of her sexuality after exhausting heterosexual possibilities. The two women form a relationship which eventually becomes sexual but Jessica finds it very difficult to admit her feelings, a problem which seems solved when she finally takes Helen as her date to her brother's wedding. Her traditional Jewish family are more intrigued than shocked, and Jessica attains new cachet in the eyes of her slick metropolitan boss, Josh (Scott Cohen). Helen now realises she is a committed lesbian but also that Jessica is not: although they live together, cuddle and are best friends, they do not have the passionate sexual relationship Helen desires, and she moves out. The closing scenes show Jessica and Helen meeting for coffee happily as friends, Helen telling her about her new girlfriend and Jessica responding with tales of a date with Josh.

While laudable in some respects in suggesting that people should be able to choose their partners regardless of labels like 'straight' and 'gay', *Kissing Jessica Stein* elects a conservative ending when it pairs its female hero with her male boss rather than her girlfriend. The film's commitment to realism here undoes the potential egalitarian tendencies which would establish lesbian relationships as equally worthy of focus within the romantic comedy as heterosexual ones. By choosing Jessica, the one-time lesbian, as the hero instead of Helen, who becomes committed to finding a woman partner, the film marginalises the very sexuality it sets out to showcase.

One final film which needs to be considered as an heir to the open or unhappy ending observable in the radical romantic comedy, again a film which flirts with the idea of gay sexuality although here attached to a supporting character, is *My Best Friend's Wedding* (1997). The film inherits the 1970s films' interest in the competing demands of romance and sex, and here finds perhaps the ultimate solution to this competition: splitting them. Jules (Julia Roberts) maintains a romantic fondness for Michael (Dermot Mulroney) whom she once dated; when she learns he is going to marry a rich young woman, Kim (Cameron Diaz), she tries to ruin the marriage plans so that she can have Michael herself. Jules is alternately aided and hindered in her scheming by her other best friend, George (Rupert Everett, in a role substantially enlarged after preview audiences demanded more of the character). Unlike the slightly rough and ready Michael, the polished George appears to offer everything a woman could hope for in a partner:

handsome, witty, completely devoted. He has one flaw, however: he is gay. The film manages to underline this and yet by the end of the film subvert it so that the very problem with George becomes his greatest asset. As Kim and Michael marry and depart on their honeymoon, Jules remains sadly at the reception. Suddenly her mobile rings: George tells her she looks lovely. She realises he is there, hunts for him amid the revellers, and is spun by George into a dance move. He is the man who will give Jules the romance she needs: he has followed her to the wedding, he is there when she needs someone, he woos her with suspense and compliments and then provides the perfection of a skilled dance partner. George acknowledges, in the film's final words, that the split between sex and romance has become final: while she must look to other men to satisfy her physical needs, Jules can be reassured that she has him to satisfy her emotional ones:

George: There may not be marriage. There may not be sex. But, by god, there'll be dancing.

My Best Friend's Wedding can be seen as aspiring to *Annie Hall*'s radicalism by ending with the female hero permanently denied the partner she wants and coupled instead with a gay man. The film very skillfully juggles the conflicting resonances of this conclusion, managing to suggest an upbeat ending even while confirming Jules' exclusion from the coupling Kim and Michael have achieved. Everett's handsome face, elegant and poised body, and playful and tender manner towards Jules provide the visual and emotional charges we expect at the end of the romantic comedy: the film looks like it has a happy conclusion, with the heroine in her lavender satin dress dancing with the handsome hero. In maintaining a final image of Jules in a couple, even if it is a non-sexual one, the film is not as radical a text as *An Unmarried Woman*, which ends with the woman alone in the cityscape, or *Annie Hall*, which ends with both lovers physically absent from the screen. We also need to question whether this ending is so liberatory: while it appears to affirm the supremacy of romance unshackled by tricky questions about sexuality, is it really that upbeat to conclude that the odd girl out ends up with no sex? That the man who is perfect for her is gay and therefore both must look elsewhere for sexual fulfilment? The gay best friend character exists as a compensatory fantasy for women who find themselves without boyfriends; this is exposed if one considers what George gets out

Figure 13: The happy couple in *My Best Friend's Wedding*.

of his relationship with Jules. If all of us need romance, where is George to get his helping from and why should it not be from his partner, who is occasionally shown in the background? While it seems that Jules must split romance and sex and rely on separate providers for these necessities, why should George, who is successfully in a long-term relationship, have to do so? George thus gets nothing from Jules but gratitude.

Baz Dreisinger (2000) argues that this gay best friend character, a stock romantic comedy figure for a time in the late 1990s, is a response to society's fears about the basic incompatibility of the sexes. The gay man is a woman's best hope of a perfect partner, because he likes shopping, shoes, eating in restaurants and dancing, as much as she does. Although obviously this is a stereotyped view of both gay men and women, this is not the only problem that the use of the gay best friend generates for the narrative. Dreisinger suggests that:

> Jules does not get Michael, but she gets something better. She gets the gay friend, the un-boyfriend who comes with all the benefits of a lover but none of the dangers. He is not the inscrutable, potentially threatening creature of self-help lore, but the only man who can successfully offer a woman all the eroticism of sex without its malevolent side-effects. (2000: 7)

The romantic comedy cannot sustain its commitment to the gay best friend as a straight woman's romantic solution, however, since if every woman followed Jules there would be no procreation and no new audience members for romantic comedies. This perhaps explains the character's increased marginalisation as the new century dawned: Melanie's gay pal Frederick (Nathan Lee Graham) in *Sweet Home Alabama* (2002) is granted much less screen time and presence than George in *My Best Friend's Wedding* or the temporary boyfriend substitutes of *The Object of My Affection* (1998) and *The Next Best Thing* (2000). The neo-traditional romantic comedies return to an insistence on the primacy of the female/male couple, but, as will be seen, without the commitment to the importance of sexual fulfilment to both genders that so marked the films from the 1970s.

THE NEO-TRADITIONAL ROMANTIC COMEDY

Accounts of the development of the romantic comedy often seem to compress the time between *Annie Hall* in 1977 and *When Harry Met Sally* in 1989 (Krutnik 1998) telescoping the twelve years between them into a single impulse begun by Allen's film and adopted by Nora Ephron, writer of *When Harry Met Sally* and writer-director of *Sleepless in Seattle* and *You've Got Mail*. The particular brand of romantic comedy grouped together is New York-based, literate, self-reflexive, and may thus appear at first fairly homogenous. However, while Allen's film differs from the others in the complexity of its structure and radical ending, Ephron's films, by contrast, prepare the viewer for this type of ending by the seemingly insurmountable odds facing the couple, only to remove these in the final reel to achieve the unlikely reconciliation.

These films, therefore, while close to *Annie Hall* in their visual elements, adopt a much more conservative and traditional ending. I call these films neo-traditional because they represent a return to a notional form of romantic comedy which they assume to have existed. The works they reference, however, come not from the ranks of screwball or sex comedies, but from romantic *dramas*, and it is from this type of film that the newer romantic comedy draws its increased emphasis on the importance of tears. While the previous chapters have each represented important topical evolutions in the romantic comedy, the neo-traditional romantic comedy is not so much a significant sub-genre as *the* dominant current form of the genre. It has defied the roughly decade-long supremacy which each of the other types of romantic comedy enjoyed, having been the major form for nearly

twenty years. It is also significant in not representing a forward development or evolution of the previous form. While each manifestation inflected
the conventions of the previous group in pursuit of its own preoccupations,
the neo-traditional romantic comedy does not take up and twist the concerns of the previous sub-genre's films: instead it acts as if movies like *The
Graduate* and *Annie Hall* never existed. The neo-traditional romantic comedy elects to ignore that films have ended with the lovers apart, or together
but possibly only temporarily. Although it keeps the appearance, inherited
from the 1970s films, of being a more realistic type of romantic comedy,
it has no use for realism if this means facing up to the actual problems of
forming a lasting relationship in contemporary society. The new form of the
romantic comedy pays lip service to such ideas as big-city alienation, the
prevalence of divorce and the inevitability of disappointment, but does so
only to confound them with the perfect romance it then produces for its
protagonists.

A definition of the neo-traditional romantic comedy stresses its return
to the conventions of earlier comedies, ignoring the elements that made
the radical romantic comedy so exciting for a time:

> The neo-traditional romantic comedy reasserts the old 'boy meets,
> loses, regains girl' structure, emphasising the couple will be hetero-
> sexual, will form a lasting relationship, and that their story will end
> as soon as they do so.

One trait of the radical romantic comedies, which these films from the late
1980s onwards maintain, is a nostalgia for earlier movies. They reference
times when, it is assumed, romance was more straightforward – what Frank
Krutnik terms a 'heterosexual arcadia' (1990: 57). There are variations in
the success of these referencings, however: whereas Woody Allen took his
inspiration for the ending of *Annie Hall* from European art films, the more
conventional romantic comedy of this period draws on older films in a much
less specific manner. *Only You* (1994) has Faith (Marisa Tomei) rejecting all
real suitors for a fantasy partner, invoking the power of Hollywood romances via *Casablanca,* and, aurally, *South Pacific* (1958) for support. The audience is expected to get the references to the older movies and realise the
kind of romantic love she seeks is old-fashioned but not impossible. This
cannibalism of elements from other romantic films seems widespread. For

example, *Kate and Leopold* seems to reference the romantic dinner Elliot prepares for Paula in *The Goodbye Girl*, repeating the heroine's surprised arrival in a transformed wonderland high above the teeming city. While Elliot himself sang to Paula, Leopold has paid a violinist to serenade their table; the fairytale *mise-en-scène* is repeated, with hundreds of candles replacing Elliot's string of Christmas tree lights. In both scenes the hero invites the heroine to muse upon previous failed romances as a prelude to realising she can form a successful couple with him. This is the occasion, however, for *Kate and Leopold*'s moment of self-appraisal as a film in a long line of others peddling an irresponsible fantasy – the 'Love Santa' moment mentioned in chapter one. Does *Kate and Leopold* reference *The Goodbye Girl* in order to indict it for similarly fostering audiences' yearnings for the perfect impractical romance, or in order to leech off any warmth of feeling remaining for the earlier film – or even just to steal its effective setting? Perhaps for all three reasons; the point of the neo-traditional romantic comedy's borrowings is difficult to discern.

While *Annie Hall* consciously evoked art cinema, *Kate and Leopold*'s motives for its referencing are unclear. Furthermore, the film's self-aware-ness in recognising that it recycles 'a grown-up version of Santa Claus' ends there: while the narrative may stall when Kate speaks of the commercial motivations behind romance, it soon judders to life again as Leopold, dis-missing her pessimism, swoops her into a waltz. Unlike Elliot and Paula's dance, which was interrupted by the rain in the film's display of its realist tendencies, Kate and Leopold's waltz remains fairytale perfect, and antici-pates the final scene of the film where Kate manages to inject herself into Leopold's century, affirming her decision to sacrifice twenty-first-century New York in order to keep hold of her perfect match.

Although *Kate and Leopold*'s 'Love Santa' moment very briefly acknow-ledges realistic consumer motivations for the contemporary romantic comedy, its commitment throughout the rest of the film is to maintaining standard myths about romance. The film reveals itself as an artefact with conflicting aims, torn between exposing the old lies and blandly trotting them out again. This self-embarrassment, observable in many contempo-rary romantic comedies, is actively countered in some films which import elements from other types of comedy, such as the 'gross-out' comedy of 'Hollywood Lowbrow' (Bonila 2005). However, the use of messy slapstick, bodily malfunctions and emphasising of sex, found at times in films such as *Along Came Polly* (2004) sits uneasily beside its more conformist moments.[1]

Contexts of the neo-traditional romantic comedy

The neo-traditional romantic comedy has lasted beyond the usual decade which bracketed the flourishing of the earlier sub-genres. Films in the now-dominant form, marked by their rejection of advances made in the radical film and a return to older conventions, have persisted since the end of the 1980s until the present time, thus spanning over fifteen years, three American presidencies and their various, varying historical and social contexts, including the full emergence of the AIDS crisis, the reassertion of 'family values', the rise of the religious right and a corresponding emphasis on sexual caution, monogamy and abstinence.

Despite the different production contexts existing over this period, there seems to be a very similar product emerging. This is a clear sign that the films are cut off from their originating times, either wilfully or by accident rejecting what is specific about their contexts, in favour of a more generalised, undifferentiated feeling. Perhaps this very obliviousness to contemporary specificities has enabled the neo-traditional romantic comedy to last so long: unlike the radical romantic comedy which can seem dated because of its references to the zeitgeist, the current dominant form of the genre prefers to reference popular culture and consumer products rather than political or historical events. Characters in *An Unmarried Woman*, for example, mention the Black Panther movement, the Vietnam War and the assassinations of the 1960s; by contrast, contemporary detailing in the neo-traditional romantic comedy runs more to the acknowledgement of elaborate coffee choices like Kathleen's 'tall skim caramel machiato' in *You've Got Mail*, and the fashion for speed-dating, referenced in *The 40 Year Old Virgin* and *Hitch* (2005).

The trend, observable in some of the 1970s films, of using the material of contemporary urban life for visual cues, rather than really embracing a radical form of romantic comedy, is maintained by these later films, becoming even more marked. Such films employ the trappings of realism but empty them of specific relevance, as is noticeable in the treatment of the cityscape, one of the most recurrent images in the contemporary romantic comedy. The neo-traditional romantic comedy aligns itself with the urban milieu, films which shun the big city and suggest the supremacy instead of the small rural backwater (*Sweet Home Alabama*) or island retreat (*50 First Dates*, 2004) being both rare and rather unconvincing. This is not to say that the use of (almost inevitably) New York in the neo-traditional romantic comedy *is* convincing: on the contrary, the city is generally referenced in such films through a selection of easily-recognised landmarks, the types of buildings, bridges and shops on any tourist's itinerary. This varies crucially from the use Woody Allen made of New York in *Annie Hall* and *Manhattan* (1979). At the point of the former's release it had become more common to note the violence of the city than its architectural or cultural beauties; a 1972 *Variety* review of a Barbra Streisand vehicle for example, noted that it subscribed to the routine view that New York was an uncomfortable city to inhabit: '[*Up the Sandbox* [1972] is] laced with by-now-boring gallows humour about how bad life is in Manhattan' (Anon. 1972). This had been a standard trope in comedies since at least *Mr Blanding Builds His Dream House* (1948), and would be reworked in blaxploitation films such as *Shaft* (1971) and *Superfly* (1972), as well as the Martin Scorsese films *Mean Streets* (1973) and *Taxi Driver*. New York was thus routinely employed in films across genres as a locale whose idiosyncrasies signalled danger rather than romance, and comedies like *The Out of Towners* (1970) gleefully detailed the miseries that unwary visitors could expect. Allen's films can be seen as responsible for the major change in the cinematic portrayal of New York: far from a place of crime and alienation, it has now become *the* location for romance, evoked so often that its mere presence in a film acts as a generic guarantee. New York is where romantic love happens: against the odds love (*Green Card*, 1990), Cinderella-style cross-class love (*Maid in Manhattan*, 2002 and *Hitch*), blue-collar love (*Moonstruck*, 1987), black love (*Brown Sugar*, 2002), lesbian love (*Kissing Jessica Stein*). The presence of the city is a warranty for the successful love story: its mere evocation in the credit sequence of *The Wedding Date* (2005), the main action of which takes place in England, is enough to confirm that the two New Yorkers Kat (Debra Messing) and Nick (Dermot Mulroney) will become a couple.

The lack of specificity in referencing noted as a trait in the neo-traditional romantic comedy is thus equally marked with regards to the city, filmmakers using recognisable visual elements of New York as shorthand to create a romantic mood, rather than to evoke specific locations. Real details of everyday life are used as *mise-en-scène*, rather than as aspects which inform the narrative, a tendency film does not share with television which, in its use of the city (as in Darren Star's *Sex and the City*, 1998–2004) is much more specific. The rote use of the city as iconography in the neo-traditional romantic comedy seems another sign that this type of film has exhausted its inspirations. Regrettably there seems to be no abatement in their number, but the homogeneity of such films indicates the need for an infusion of new characteristics, if the genre is going to survive. Abandoning the possibility of revealing that life continues after the final clinch, which the 1970s radical romantic comedy so enjoyed exploring, the neo-traditional romcom thus demonstrates how much ground it has given up. While *The Heartbreak Kid* could start with one wedding and ironically end with another, with the same groom, films such as *How to Lose a Guy in 10 Days* and *Animal Attraction* (2001) do not have the confidence to depict the couple after their final reel reconciliation; *You've Got Mail*, considered below, seems so doubtful about the plausibility of its protagonists' love that it confines their union to the very last moments of the film.

Characteristics of the neo-traditional romantic comedy

Again there are both overarching themes recurring in the films being grouped together here, and more micro-tropes of visuality and music frequently repeat also. One of the most obvious traits is the overdetermination of romantic signifiers used in the films' titles. As if afraid that their various marketing teams might fail to saturate the target audiences with trailers, adverts, television spots and other publicity to create interest in the pictures, the film titles themselves parade their romantic comedy status, usually either referencing romantic relationships, the city, or confirming the primacy of the couple. Thus recent films have stressed the inevitability of the successful coupling by using the word 'wedding' – *The Wedding Singer* (1998), *The Wedding Planner* (2001), *The Wedding Date, My Best Friend's Wedding, My Big Fat Greek Wedding* (2002); by invoking a city, the prime location of love – *LA Story* (1991), *Sleepless in Seattle, Maid in Manhattan*; or by linking a man and woman's name – *When Harry Met Sally, Kate and Leopold, Alex and Emma* (2003). With the stars they employ and the iconography the posters use, there is never any doubt such films are romantic comedies: underlining this obvious fact by the title seems to indicate an anxiety within the genre itself. Like the aura of embarrassment pervading so many modern romantic comedies, this anxiety has at its root feelings of the genre's obsolescence and irrelevance to contemporary life.

This underlying anxiety can be seen to drive many of the characteristics common to these films. Just as various forms of self-reflexivity, differently inflected, directed the radical romantic comedy of the 1970s, this awareness of the genre's sell-by date, looming or already past, propels the shared elements of the neo-traditional romantic comedies. These can be seen to include:

- a backlash against the ideologies of the radical film alongside a maintenance of its visual surfaces
- a mood of imprecise nostalgia
- a more vague self-referentialism
- a de-emphasising of sex

While working to evoke the world of *Annie Hall* or *Manhattan* in their visual elements, these films do not merely ignore the advances in the genre that these romantic comedies represent: they reject them. The willingness to leave even a vaguely open ending has totally gone; instead there must be no ambiguity about the reunion of the couple, it must be displayed, even if there remain many doubts about their real suitability together. For example, even though they have deceived each other, Andie and Ben from *How to Lose a Guy in 10 Days* must be seen to reconcile before the film ends. Ben chases Andie's taxi as she leaves the city, catching up with her on the Manhattan Bridge. Andie insists she wants to leave, but Ben, invoking a game they played earlier, exclaims 'Bullshit!', and the pair go into a clinch. This ending seems so forced, as the camera soars away emphasising the skyline of New York behind them, that the unconvinced viewer is likely to echo Ben's exclamation. This closed-down ending makes that of radical romantic comedy *An Unmarried Woman* seem very transgressive by contrast: even though the viewer is fairly sure Erica and Saul will get back together, the film is content enough with her independence to let Saul leave the frame, and to end with Erica alone, albeit weighed down by his painting, struggling but coping with the situation, amidst the bustle of the city.[2]

The exhausted energy of these neo-traditional films reveals itself in this insistence on recycling the visual and musical heritage of the 1970s films, the inevitable use of the cityscape and lush romantic scores from Gerswhin and Porter initiated in the Allen films, coupled with its firm rejection of the edgier qualities of these films (see also Garwood 2000). Neo-traditional romantic comedies seem, for example, afraid of the freedom offered by a more open ending and react against it as they present couples forming despite seemingly insurmountable barriers to their union – barriers geographical (*Sleepless in Seattle*), emotional *(Sweet Home Alabama)*, chronological (*Kate and Leopold*) and even mortal (in *Just Like Heaven*, 2005, one of the protagonists may be dead). In rejecting the freedoms offered by the radical romantic comedies' endings, the new form of the genre reveals its anxiety over the possibility of lasting love in contemporary society, its very relentlessness in having this as the end of every film betraying its own lack of faith in such an outcome.

While the 1970s film invoked romantic classics such as *Casablanca* and Judy Garland movies, the later film's use of *The Goodbye Girl* is much more nebulous. Watching Elliot in his white tuxedo adopting a voice and attitude, the viewer knows he is quoting someone, even if unsure exactly who. But *Kate and Leopold*, although borrowing the earlier film's romantic dinner, does not directly refer to it or acknowledge it has borrowed anything, tapping into a general sense of what is 'romantic' but without confessing its sources. The general sense of old-fashioned romance can then accrue to Leopold, the man thrust ahead of his own time by a century, who can therefore be expected to espouse older notions, even if in reality marriage was seen as a matter of dynastic business rather than emotional importance in the nineteenth century. This gesturing to a more romantic past, unanchored by specific references, marks the nostalgia of the neo-traditional romantic comedy; furthermore, it seems significant that this nostalgia is for the viewer's benefit rather than the character's. Whereas Paula, in *The Goodbye Girl*, admits the effect Elliot's efforts have on her – 'I'm a sucker for romance!' – the creation of the fairytale *mise-en-scène* in *Kate and Leopold* is for the viewer's benefit more than Kate's: it is *we* who are supposed to be the sucker for romance, and the film seems to admit this since *her* response to the romantic overload of music, candlelight, dinner and attention is to muse about the consumerist impulses fostered by the idea of love.

This seems to be one of the main tactics by which the neo-traditional romantic comedy seeks to achieve its various effects: by creating feelings in the audience it then ascribes to the characters. By this means, the hard work of establishing character traits becomes unnecessary; much more simply a song, a landmark, or a line of dialogue with an already-established emotional resonance can be employed to evoke a feeling which then gets co-opted into the new movie. This method works because audiences are very cine-literate and can be counted upon to have absorbed a certain number of such resonances, but it seems dishonest to evoke a nostalgic glow in the viewer which is then diegetically ascribed to a character. While the nostalgic referencing in Allen's *Annie Hall* was a homage to early 1960s European art classics, the audience encouraged to feel sophisticated if catching the allusions, the point of contemporary referencing is that generic rather than specific sources will be recognised. While *Kate and Leopold* seems clearly (if silently) to borrow from *The Goodbye Girl*, evocation of mood through less definite sources is observable in many other neo-traditional romantic comedies. This vague unanchored warmth for older forms of the genre is, for example, tapped into in *The Wedding Planner*, which struggles to assert the primacy of the Mary/Steve (Jennifer Lopez/Matthew McConaughey) couple by borrowing magic from older films. The pair are established as a perfect match, despite his impending marriage to another, when they dance together beautifully; being able to move together in harmony in the dance, even if fighting outside it, was a standard motif of the classical Hollywood musical (as in *The Band Wagon*, 1953) which foretold the successful establishment of the couple. The film underlines dance as a metaphor for the Mary and Steve relationship both in this moment and when couple dance together again at an open-air movie event. Going together to see a romantic classic, the pair are self-reflexively endowed with the same status as the lovers on-screen. Significantly, the filmmakers use a comic musical to confer legitimacy as a couple. The little-seen *Two Tickets to Broadway* (1951), which is never acknowledged verbally within the dialogue, provides a dance scene which generically conveys heterosexual romance accomplished through dance. Using an obscure film instead of a recognisable one as a comparison point for the pair allows their confirmation as destined lovers without subjecting them, possibly, to comparison with well-known performers of greater charisma.

Not all the neo-traditional romcoms avoid the 1970s-style overt referencing of older sources. Fred Schepisi's *Roxanne* (1987) enjoys playing with the classical love story of Cyrano de Bergerac, while permitting a contemporary happy ending to replace the hero's death which concludes the original nineteenth-century play. *Moonstruck* and *Pretty Woman* draw on nineteenth-century classical operas for their references, demonstrating in both cases the emotional transformation of the heroine as she responds to the tragic death of Mimi in *La Bohème* in the former film, and *La Traviata*'s Violetta in the latter. Several romantic comedies from the 1990s onwards have used the works of Jane Austen for their material, whether portrayed straight in bonnets and bustles (*Emma*, 1996) or adapted to modern dress (*Clueless*, 1995).

Nora Ephron's films are confident enough not to need to draw on such high cultural sources for their resonances. Using more middle-brow references to popular culture, her works very cleverly blend the employment of acknowledged, even highlighted, sources, such as *An Affair to Remember* (1947), repeatedly referenced in *Sleepless in Seattle*, with the usual much more vague and undifferentiated nostalgia generally found in the current evolution of the genre. The discussion of *You've Got Mail*, below, details some instances of direct quotation and less anchored referencing meant to evoke feelings in the viewer subsequently ascribed to the characters. This might be defended as an attempt at fostering viewer/character identification, but seems more a type of sleight of hand designed to create the appearance of in-depth characterisation without the work.

As seen, in the radical romantic comedy film of the 1970s, the most marked tendency was self-referentiality, the films' acknowledging their own awareness of themselves as romantic comedies within traditions, and both affection and frustration towards the way romantic love had been traditionally portrayed. How has this self-reflexivity evolved in more recent films? Since ironic, detached self-awareness has become a major (indeed, somewhat over-used) trait of contemporary culture – what is generally called a 'postmodern' quality, when the narrative is aware of itself as a fiction and with mock-weariness seems to declare, 'I know this is all nonsense but here it is anyway' – it is to be expected that the kind of self-referentiality fostered by the 1970s films will not have vanished, and indeed, there are many moments in the neo-traditional romantic comedy where the narrative seems to stop and take a bow, overtly acknowledging itself as an artefact (see King 2002: 62). Significantly, however, current romantic comedies do not seem to be seeking to improve upon their inspirations in terms of increased realism, but merely to evoke them to share any left-over romantic charge they may carry. A comparison of two examples illustrates the difference of the self-referentiality between the radical and neo-traditional films.

In *What's Up, Doc?*, Howard Bannister, his well-ordered life beginning to unravel since he met Judy Maxwell, wanders away from his destroyed hotel room and finds himself on the uncompleted top floor of the hotel. Here he finds a large shape covered in a dust sheet which, unveiled, proves to be a grand piano – with Judy reclining voluptuously on top. When Howard finds her, Judy calmly invokes *Casablanca*, murmuring, 'Of all the gin joints in all the towns in all the world...', before singing the familiar romantic tune from the film, 'You Must Remember This'. The film's reference to the older romantic film is part-homage, part self-mockery: Judy is aware they are not in a gin joint and, since she is stalking Howard, his arrival in her vicinity is no matter of luck. The self-referentiality of the film is tied very closely to the character of Judy who makes herself the hero of the scene by appropriating Bogart's line and style of delivery. While the line may act as a cue to a song, which could be expected given Streisand's established musical stardom, her employment of the line is perfectly in keeping with her character in the film: witty, seductive, self-aware.

By contrast, when Suzy in *Sleepless in Seattle* overtly draws the viewer's attention to *An Affair to Remember*, as mentioned in the introduction, the self-reflexivity seems more forced. The film has displayed the female protagonist, Annie, repeatedly watching this film and crying over its love story. While Sam dismisses Suzy's emotional view, the viewer is being invited to remember the older movie with fondness, to smile at easily-moved Suzy, but perhaps also to share the prickle of tears at the film's nearly tragic conclusion. The chief emotion this referencing seeks to generate is nostalgic sentiment, marked by tears, for the love affair portrayed in the older film, rather than the seductive excitement which Streisand's invocation of *Casablanca* produces within *What's Up, Doc?*

Ephron's invocation of *An Affair to Remember* may seem calculating in its attempt to co-opt emotions accrued to the earlier film for the new one, but at least *Sleepless in Seattle* does not declare itself more clever than its source. *Down With Love*, however, does just this: it tries to be witty and self-reflexive in its use of characters, plot lines, settings and costumes inspired by 1950s sex comedies such as the Doris Day/Rock Hudson movies, but reveals disdain instead of affection for such films. It uses *Pillow Talk* and *Lover Come Back* as sources for its comedy, believing itself more clued-in than its inspirations. The visual quotation extends to obviously artificial sets and overblown costumes, intended to indicate an awareness of the originals' lack of realism, but *Down With Love* also employs the split-screen technique used to genuine comic effect in *Pillow Talk*. The 1959 film used the device to display Jan and Brad whenever they were on the phone together; when Jan appears as a wedge between Brad and Irene, it both confirms her immediate interruption of the playboy's wooing and her eventual status as Brad's lover. *Down With Love* by contrast does not bother to use the device to forecast the narrative, but uses it for innuendoes, revealing the superiority it feels to its sources through using its split-screen tele-

Figures 14 and 15: *Down With Love*'s unsubtle use of split-screen

phone scene to suggest not separate spaces, but continuous ones, joined via a variety of sexual manoeuvrings.

This mention of sex brings us to the final characteristic which the contemporary neo-traditional romantic comedy exhibits: a markedly different attitude to sex from any of its forerunners. The screwball comedy derived much of its energy from erotic tensions between the female and male protagonists, conveyed in insults and physical violence; the 1950s sex comedy took advantage of changes in the Production Code and in public awareness of female sexuality to discuss sex more overtly; and the 1970s radical films made a realistic awareness of the importance of fulfilled sexuality to both partners one of their central tenets. The current form of the romantic comedy, by contrast, greatly de-emphasises sexuality. This provides a real problem for the contemporary film since it is frequently devoted to depicting modern dating habits, which realistically must include sex. Neo-traditional romcoms have to work hard to find ways to explain why sex is not happening for its main couple, unless they are teenagers (as in *A Lot Like Love*, 2005). Teen romances seem more prepared to admit a physical imperative towards sex, a point the neo-traditional films, which generally feature older characters, tacitly acknowledge by implying that sex is a somewhat immature preoccupation.

Rather than stressing the necessity of sexual fulfilment, the newer romantic comedies hint at the importance of a more vague intensity in the relationship. Annie in *Sleepless in Seattle*, for example, shares a bed with her fiancé Walter, but they are significantly not seen having sex or even cuddling intimately. Annie's mother recalls that the instant she touched her future husband's hand she knew they would have a passionate sex life: it is evident from Annie's facial response that she does not experience this sexual electricity with Walter. Because she and Sam only finally get together at the very end of the film, there is no time to discover if the couple will have this passion, but the film hints they will through the intensity of the stares which the pair exchange.

Similarly, in *You've Got Mail*, both Kathleen and Joe have a live-in partner, but neither couple is ever seen having sex, despite bedroom scenes depicting them going to bed. Sleeping is apparently all they do there, however: whatever is happening in their overt relationships, it is clearly not as exciting as the clandestine email correspondence. No sex with Joe is thus more fulfilling for Kathleen than sex with Frank; this downgrading of the importance of sex is greatly in contrast to the significance it attained as an index of individuality in the 1970s films. Even when Erica, in *An Unmarried Woman*, goes to bed with unsuitable Charlie (Cliff Gorman), the viewer is urged to applaud her for taking control of her own life. This sense of sexuality being vital to the individual's maturity and growth has definitely vanished from the newer form of the romantic comedy: instead of sexual experience being a route to self-discovery, now sexual *abstinence* is posited as more responsible, until the 'right one' comes along.

The neo-traditional romcom can encounter difficulties in trying to reconcile a surface realism about contemporary dating habits and sexual mores with this larger project of insisting sex is meaningful only within a committed relationship. *How to Lose a Guy in 10 Days*, for example, attempts to gain points for realism by exposing how routinely a dinner date becomes a sexual encounter. However, because Ben's hidden agenda is to make Andie fall in love with him, he holds back from sex, assuming she will feel more romantic if he seems to respect her. In the middle section of the film, where the couple really fall in love, they do finally have sex, in the bathroom at his parents' house. The scene is set with the couple kissing and undressing but then the shot discreetly fades away, not prying on their intimacy. While sex does occur narratively, it is not dwelt upon to the same detail as in the 1970s films where sexual incompatibilities were used for humour, just like the other parts of romantic love: *Annie Hall*, *Starting Over* and *An Unmarried Woman*, for example, all allow an unwavering camera to linger on sexual encounters, conveying the embarrassment which mismatched, or even mutual, desire can bring.

Even in *A Lot Like Love*, which more realistically portrays sexual relations coming first and the couple's interest in and eventual love of one another only dawning after some years, the youthful sexual encounter Emily (Amanda Peet) and Oliver (Aston Kutcher) have on the plane is portrayed as irresponsible, immature. As the film advances in yearly chapters, the pair come closer together emotionally but attain this closeness at the expense of their sexual relationship: subsequent sex again results in their splitting up. Though they kiss by the end of the film, there is no sense of recapturing their initial sexual delight. Rapturous sex is thus portrayed as something immature, something *not* a lot like love, which the film implies is based more on shared conversation, disappointments and compromises than heady physical pleasure.

Example of the neo-traditional romantic comedy: You've Got Mail

Nora Ephron's 1998 film, *You've Got Mail*, is a useful example of the current evolution of the romantic comedy, demonstrating the characteristics common to the contemporary generic form, and also attesting the effectiveness of these characteristics in evoking emotions from the audience.

The film skillfully blends overtly acknowledged inspirations with more vague borrowings; it employs that undifferentiated nostalgia which seeks to evoke an emotion in the viewer through association, rather than through characterisation or plot development. The film is also aware of its own textual status, alluding to previous forms of the romantic comedy. Overwhelmingly, *You've Got Mail* strives for the visual and aural textures of the radical romantic comedy, via the inevitable New York locations and use of old-fashioned romantic tunes, but the ideology of those films is overturned. *You've Got Mail* does not permit itself either the possibility of an even remotely open ending, or any emphasis on the importance of sexual fulfilment, both of which marked the 1970s generic form.

While the film seeks to locate itself in the tradition of the New York-based romantic comedy, its references to a particular location – very specifically, the Upper West Side of Manhattan – are coupled with an imprecise, tourist-like use of the city. Nothing is displayed that is not picturesque or whimsical, the entire city becoming condensed to a few streets bustling with fruit and flower markets, parks, delicatessens and Starbucks. The aural patterns of the 1970s romantic comedy, with its use of traditional romantic songs, is sometimes followed. This is evident in the use of the Louis Armstrong track 'The Dummy Song', comically insulting the beloved, which occurs during the battling of the main characters, Kathleen Kelly and Joe Fox. A modern rendering of the wishful song 'Somewhere Over the Rainbow' from *The Wizard of Oz* (1939) is also used, tapping into the theme of wishing running throughout the script and musical choices, but also tacitly referencing the well-loved classic film. The multiple work done by this song indicates the film's tactic of creating feelings through a purposefully unspecific nostalgia.

Besides the picturesque locations in New York, which the film generally photographs in rich golden light, it also makes use of seasonal changes (crisp autumn leaves, falling snow, spring blossom) to mark the passing of time but more fundamentally to create in the viewer an emotional response, redoubled by the foregrounding of cosy, family-based festivals as major backdrops to the narrative's events. Kathleen and Joe first meet around Thanksgiving, in November, as the cheerful orange pumpkins and turkey motifs testify; Kathleen worries about her shop's failure around Christmas, as she decorates the shop tree with home-made decorations, and snow softly falls outside. When Joe realises he loves Kathleen, it is spring, with blue skies, fluffy clouds and pink blossom everywhere, and by the time they finally meet as lovers the summer flowers are blooming in Riverside Park. The growing warmth of their feelings echoes the warmth of the seasons: they fight and are sad in the cold months and warm to each other as the weather improves. Moreover, the film tries to absorb the traditional warm feelings associated with the seasonal festivities itself. Nostalgic appreciation for one's own childhood Christmases is then evoked by Kathleen's use of home-made tree ornaments; her missing her mother especially at Christmas reminds viewers of times beyond recall.

The film's employment of this type of sleight of hand, co-opting feelings evoked by other means and absorbing them into the narrative, can also be seen by the emphasis on the importance of familial relationships: Kathleen is very aware of her shop as her mother's legacy, and indeed nostalgia is associated especially with Kathleen. Her character is built around valuing the old, the traditional, the classical. The key line of dialogue revealing this comes early in the film: when Joe and Kathleen have just met in her shop, the little girl he is escorting sneezes, and Kathleen produces for her a cotton handkerchief, 'a Kleenex that you don't throw away'. The message is very clear: Joe lives in a world where things are disposed of once used, where endless resources mean endlessly restockable supplies. Kathleen by contrast has been taught the old-fashioned value of thrift: why throw the handkerchief away when it can be laundered and re-used? Underlining the importance of permanence versus the instantly replaceable is the fact that Kathleen's mother embroidered the handkerchief with her daughter's initials and favourite flower. Her preference for the old and established extends to her taste in reading and home comforts: *Pride and Prejudice* is a favourite book, and she yearns for cocoa and curls up under a patchwork quilt when miserable. Unlike the ardour of her unsuitable boyfriend for the typewriter, as opposed to the laptop computer, this preference is not fetishistic, based on the objects themselves, but nostalgic, resulting from the emotional memories the objects evoke.

A similarly non-specific warmth is meant to be generated by the film references which *You've Got Mail* employs. While some of its allusions are direct – the quotations from *The Godfather* (1972), for example, and the use of the name 'The Shop Around the Corner' for Kathleen's bookstore, which cites the film's source, the 1940 Ernst Lubitsch film – others are less precise. The most obvious of these is *Sleepless in Seattle*: the reteaming of the male and female lead with the director of their former great success acts as a guarantee of the film's highly sentimental agenda. Even less specifically, the film evokes at moments different evolutions of the romantic comedy, with some sequences reminiscent of the screwball, and others closer to the sex comedy.

For example, the film's beginning reveals Kathleen rushing to check her email. Meg Ryan's performance underlines the clandestine nature of the correspondence by the surreptitious manner in which she tiptoes around her apartment, checking Frank has really left before logging on. Her exaggerated physical gestures in tiptoeing, peeking and getting a message are all evocative of the screwball genre, and this resonance is strengthened by repeating the scene with Joe and his partner Patricia. The slapstick style of humour associated with screwball comedy is further found when Joe falls off the treadmill at his gym hearing Kathleen insult him on television.

Figure 16: *You've Got Mail*'s clandestine correspondents: Kathleen…

Figure 17: ...and Joe

Such pratfalls were common in the screwball and though restricted to this incident in *You've Got Mail*, deriving humour from physical and facial facets of the actors' performance continues throughout the film. The sex comedy is referenced in scenes where Joe and Kathleen insult each other. These draw on the energy of similar word battles in sex comedies such as *Pillow Talk*, although lacking that film's enjoyment of sexualised innuendo.

The film's similarity to, and simultaneous distance from, films in the radical romantic comedy tradition is illustrated by the pictures opposite: while visually similar, narratively the couples are very different. Annie and Alvy sit on their park bench cosily enjoying this moment in public alongside other moments of private intimacy together; Kathleen and Joe have only the public moments. *You've Got Mail* chooses to dwell on the courtship process of romance, like the older forms of comedy, rather than interrogate the relationship stage, as the radical *Annie Hall* does, perhaps as a necessary consequence of its de-emphasis of sexual matters.

This last characteristic of the neo-traditional romantic comedy is very noticeable in the Ephron film. Not only do Joe and Kathleen remain for all the movie at the courtship stage, only finally coming together for a kiss in the very last moments of the film, but they also seem in sexless relationships with their other partners, as their bedroom wear and behaviour attest. Ryan seems cute rather than sensuous in masculine, oversized pyjamas; though Patricia is seen in more sexy satin bedwear, she falls asleep snoring in bed. Contact between the two couples is playful at best, and more often perfunctory: there is no kissing. The most erotic moments occur when Joe and Kathleen email each other whilst both sitting on their beds, a parity which suggests they may eventually end up in bed together, and again when he actually touches her, putting his hand across her mouth to stop

Figure 18: Intimacy and distance: *Annie Hall*...

Figure 19: ...and *You've Got Mail*

her insulting him again. Both seem aware of, and rather embarrassed by, the physical intimacy implicit in this gesture. This embarrassment with intimacy is not something felt by the characters alone, but, seemingly, drives the film itself, which presents the romance of the film in remarkably non-sexual terms, as the film's opening establishes.

The whimsical 'Puppy Song', sung by Harry Nilson, plays over the title credits and the now-inevitable scenes of the New York cityscape. As the camera traverses the city streets, zoning in successively on one building, one floor, one window, one room and then eventually finding one person, Kathleen, who is in bed asleep, the words of the song seem to speak directly of her desires. This is achieved especially through the tune's connection of wishes with dreams, and the assignment of these dreams and wishes to Kathleen, when the song and the roving camera both find their destination in her. What Kathleen is dreaming about and wishing for is not the sexual partner longed for by Jan, in the words of the title song of *Pillow Talk* ('a pillow-talking boy'), but something much more tame, a desire more a- or pre-sexual:

> If only I could have a puppy, I'd call myself so very lucky
> Just to have some company, to share a cup of tea with me.
> I'd take my puppy everywhere (la la la la) I wouldn't care,
> We'd stay away from crowds, the signs that say No Dogs Allowed,
> Oh-ee, I know he'd never bite me...
>
> If only I could have a friend, to stick with me until the end
> And walk along beside the sea, to share a bit of moon with me.
> I'd take my friend most everywhere (la la la la) I wouldn't care,
> We'd stay away from crowds, the signs that say No Friends Allowed,
> Oh-ee, oh how happy we'd be...
>
> But dreams are nothing more than wishes and a wish is just a
> dream you wish to come true...

While the lyrics of the song may be difficult to make out as the viewer is occupied wondering where the roaming camera is going to go, the words 'puppy' and 'friend' are repeated often enough, along with the lines about dreams and wishes, for these terms to sink in, and they are very soon picked up visually as the film commences. The message we see Kathleen receive from her anonymous email pal is about his dog, Brinkley. As she reads the message aloud, Meg Ryan's voice is replaced by Tom Hanks's, and the scene shifts from her apartment to his, where we see the dog he is telling her about. Within the opening few minutes, then, there is the establishment of a yearning for a dog and a friend, the association of this yearning with Kathleen, and the suggestion of the eventual identities of this dog and friend. The fulfilment of these wishes comes at the end of the film when 'NY152' (Joe) emails 'Shopgirl' (Kathleen) to say that he and Brinkley will meet her in Riverside Park. As Kathleen waits anxiously she hears the dog bark, its name being called, and then sees Joe arriving. Her emotional investment in her email pen-pal has been confirmed throughout the film by the importance the correspondence has for Kathleen, her willingness to give up Frank without having found someone else already, but with 'the dream of someone else' sustaining her. Kathleen's dreams of romantic involvement with this someone merge with her dream of having a puppy and a friend at the film's conclusion, where the important personae peopling her world – business rival-turned-friend, pen-friend and potential husband – turn out to be the same dog-owning person, Joe Fox. The neo-traditional romantic comedy film's downgrading of the importance of sex to the characters is clearly evidenced by the lack of any erotic contact between the two eventual lovers; indeed, the only character portraying desire is Joe's 'wicked stepmother', Gillian (Cara Seymour), whose attempts to seduce him make him obviously uncomfortable. Gillian's predatory sexuality marks her as a bad woman, as Kathleen's vague unsexualised longings of a dream partner with whom to discuss books, music and New York, confirm her the contemporary heroine.

CONCLUSION

The current form of the Hollywood romantic comedy is apparently aware of its own impoverishment and exhaustion. There seems to be a crisis of faith in the products of the genre strikingly evident in the great industry surprise when a romantic comedy does well at the box office. It is to be hoped that this 'last days' feeling truly does mark the end of the current cycle of reused images and soundtracks; certainly there needs to be an infusion of new elements if the genre is going to be able to regain credibility. In order to move forward and remain a viable genre, the romantic comedy will need to throw off some of its current tendencies and adopt new ones.

Three main themes seem to be emerging which counter the current form of the genre: a re-emphasis on the importance of sex; a positioning of a man instead of a woman as the centre of the narrative; and a willingness to use the now-habitual overworn elements of the romcom as an occasion for parody. In examining these possible new directions we return to the ideas about audiences, emotions and self-reflexivity with which this book began.

While the latter tendency, the willingness to acknowledge and laugh at, rather than just re-use, the tropes of the genre, can be seen in films from the 1990s onwards, as in *Denise Calls Up* (1995) and *The Daytrippers* (1996), these were independent productions making fun of mainstream products for their own marginal, hip audiences, rather than mainstream products themselves. With *Date Movie* (2006), however, the urge to parody generic elements arrived firmly in the multiplex rather than the art-house. Significantly, *Date Movie*, directed by one of the writers behind the successful *Scary Movie* franchise, was targeted, like the horror parodies, at a much younger audience than is usually assumed for romantic comedies. The success of the film's quotations of moments from romcoms including *My Big Fat Greek Wedding, When Harry Met Sally, Hitch, The Wedding Planner* and *What Women Want* (2000) and many others, depends on the audience's recognition of the citations, so the film can be seen assuming that, despite being outside the traditional demographic for such films, the intended youthful audience will have familiarity with these romantic comedies. Similarly, *My Super Ex-Girlfriend* (2006) blends the superhero film and romcom to poke fun at both cycles, again exploiting a younger audience's insider knowledge of hallowed romcom characteristics.

Less slapstick employment of the usual romcom elements can also be seen in contemporary movies made for more traditional (assumed female[1]) audiences: both *Monster-in-Law* (2005) and *Prime* (2006) reveal a self-reflexive awareness of genre tropes in re-organising their trajectories so that the typical sparring at the heart of the romcom goes on not between the woman and the man, but the woman and the man's *mother*. Generating invigorating comic performances by the twin female leads (Jane Fonda and Jennifer Lopez in the former film; Meryl Streep and Uma Thuman in the latter), these movies speak knowingly to their assumed audiences of women about the importance of female relationships, ensuring the sizzle in the dialogue and performances is generated by the women through casting male leads who are attractive but bland. Further address to a knowing and clued-in audience is made by the British *Bridget Jones* films; as Madelyn Ritrosky-Winslow (2006) elegantly demonstrates in an article about the films' intertextuality, the specific pleasures of female audience members were courted and catered to by the female writing-directing teams responsible for the movies.

Diane Negra, in an article for online journal *Flow*, considers the male-centred comedy, noting a rise in the last few years of films 'about the uncoupled thirty- or forty-something male and his failure to take up his proper role in the social order' (2006: 1). It is true that the 1970s radical films did not feel themselves constrained to concentrate on either women characters, or assume a predominantly female audience: *Starting Over, The Heartbreak Kid* and indeed *Annie Hall*, which is easily as much about Alvy Singer as Annie herself, clearly illustrate this, indicating these films' awareness of romantic love being as important to men as to women. But this contemporary re-emergence of the central male character demonstrates the great distance the conventional neo-traditional romantic comedy has put between itself and its immediate generic predecessor: the current form of the genre seems to have been almost inevitably both associated with, marketed to and centred on, women: 'most romantic comedies are aimed at us girls' (Berry & Errigo 2004: 38).

For about ten years now, however, there has been a counter tendency to devote the attention of the romantic comedy to the male protagonist. In this small cycle of films, other elements – the emphasis on city life, on the difficulties of trying to find the right one amongst the unsuitable many, former disappointments and current possibilities of success – are all repeated. The object of this maintenance of core elements around the changed gender of the central character is to confirm that men need romance too. In the better-balanced neo-traditional films (Ephron's are good examples), both the man and woman yearn for the right partner; in these newer 'romcoms for boys', or, as we might call them, *hommecoms*, the films work to counterbalance all those other narratives which have depicted only the central females' longing.

Interestingly, the films which centre on the yearning male, from *Swingers* (1996) to *Hitch,* also devote themselves first to suggesting, then denying, that there is a proper structure to romance: a set of rules. As the male protagonists of the earlier films discuss how many days to wait before calling a girl, so the self-styled 'date doctor' of the more recent work begins the movie by addressing the audience directly about the rules of modern relationships, even if he ends it by acknowledging, 'there are no rules'.

Similarly, the mystical code of cool embodied by three Steves (McGarrett, of *Hawaii 5-0*; Austin, of *The Six Million Dollar Man*; and McQueen) is supposed to account for the hero's extraordinary success with women in *The Tao of Steve* (2000). Dex (Donal Logue) is not conventionally attractive, being overweight, much given to alcohol, loafing and avoiding commitment. Adopting the code of cool thus seemingly helps him achieve sexual success with women who would otherwise dismiss him; this devil-may-care attitude to sex is implicitly condemned when, at the end, Dex seems to have matured enough to abandon the code to be with just one woman.

This presentation of bed-hopping as immature continues in *Wedding Crashers* (2005). Its central protagonists John (Owen Wilson) and Jeremy (Vince Vaughn) are exhibited in an early montage of weddings employing their code of behaviour: turn up at a wedding masquerading as a distant relative, pick a target, then select a technique to woo her from a list of several routines calculated to indicate the man's soft heart and romantic nature (dancing with the six-year-old bridesmaid, crying at the wedding service). The culmination of each routine is impressive dancing, with the target seductively twirled to the music. The montage illustrates each woman beginning the twirl upright in her wedding outfit and ending it falling backwards onto a bed in her lingerie, clearly revealing the ultimate aim of the male pair is casual sex. Again, however, this immature attitude to sexual encounters is demonstrated to be wrong, and for a time splits up the male friends, as John begins to tire of the endless pretence, falls for just one girl and renounces their operating code. Jeremy appears to resent this but secretly he too has fallen in love, and the film ends at *his* wedding with the reconciliation both of the male friends and of John and his beloved.

In each of these male-centred romantic comedies a framework is thus established at the beginning of the film which provides the rules of romance. Although each of these frameworks is obviously meant to provide part of the humour of the romantic comedy, and not meant seriously as a life-guide, each of the films takes pains to underline that adherence to the code is immature and ultimately unhelpful, and all end by demonstrating the abandonment of the rules. This emphasis on rules and codes for love does not seem to be abating: the book, *Jane Austen's Guide to Dating* (2005), which seems intent to tap into the dual popularity of Austen's works and the notion of rules for love, despite offering a how-to guide rather than a narrative, has been optioned to become a film (Betts 2005). What this interest in the codes of romance indicates is an overwhelming awareness of the *lack* of rules for love. Obviously love itself has not significantly changed, but our tolerance of the uncertainties pertaining to love seem to have done so. While the radical movies of the 1970s gained energy from the fluidity of erotic emotions and the transience of affection, the current neo-traditional romantic comedies take only anxiety from these ideas.

Anxiety seems to lie also at the root of the *hommecom* cycle. These films set out to prove the male hero can be as sensitive, as heartsick and desperate for love as the female. Similarly, other films such as *The Sweetest Thing* (2002) and portions of *The Wedding Date* reverse the equation to indicate girls can be as coarse, sex-obsessed and keen for drunken fun as boys; such films tap into a contemporary social phenomenon that writer Ariel Levy (2005) claims represents a new 'Raunch Culture', part of a wider pattern of self-objectifying by women whom she terms 'Female Chauvinist Pigs' (see also Cochrane 2006). Such films set out to insist the initial differences between the sexes can be overcome because, in the boy films, all THEY (men) really want too is passionate sex in a committed loving relationship, just like WE (women) do, and in the 'bad girl' ones, WE just want fun and sex and drink just like THEY do. Far from tapping in to a lessening of the gender divide, however, this insistence on the similarity of the sexes seems instead to underline a real fear that the differences between men and women are either getting worse or have always been ineradicable.

With the final current counter tendency, the re-emphasis on sex, some contemporary films are trying to acknowledge both the primacy of the importance of this area of human experience and its inherent humour. *The 40 Year Old Virgin* contains many scenes of sexual encounters gone wrong: amidst the candles and seductive music, the hero always injures himself or his partner. This film is not afraid to depict how ugly the human being intent on sex can be: the contorted faces of Andy's partners as they try with frustration to gain pleasure provoke humour rather than arouse. The film's emphasis on the simultaneous importance and ridiculousness of sex co-opts slapstick elements to provoke humour and to present a more realistic worldview, but its ending still supplies heterosexual monogamy as the answer to Andy's problematic virginity. After marrying Trish (Catherine Keener) Andy finally gets to experience sex. Although this first encounter is over within a minute, Andy's long-stored stock of sexual energy enables him to try again immediately, this time for two hours, until Trish is clearly sated. Andy then looks directly into the camera from bed and begins to sing 'Aquarius', from the 1968 musical *Hair*. This song promotes a general idea about newly-dawning awareness, a euphoric awakening which testifies to the significance of Andy's first partnered sexual experiences. As the song becomes a production number with the other characters joining in, running and leaping about in a sunny meadow, the implication could be that sex in a properly loving, committed relationship can be as blissful, as beneficial to the entire universe, as the golden period of harmony brought about by astrological alignment ('When the Moon is in the seventh house, and Jupiter aligns with Mars/Then Peace will guide the planets, and Love will steer the stars').

However, it is also possible to advance a reading which links the use of this song at the end of the film to the general tendency in current romantic comedies to downplay the primacy of sexual experience. The song comes from a period of multiple drug use and multiple sexual partners, both of which are celebrated in the 1960s musical, and both of which Andy has never known. This, coupled with the fact that all his formerly rampant male colleagues appear at the wedding neatly paired off or even more securely wedged into familial stability by having children, can be seen to redirect the original thrust of the song, which encourages the listener to seek sexual enlightenment. The message now seems to be that true freedom comes from being in a relationship, not as an individual thinking of her/his own pleasures. This is definitely to reverse the original context of the song but seems in keeping with the current downgrading of the importance of *personal* sexual fulfilment within film representation. Even in films such as *The 40 Year Old Virgin* and *Wedding Crashers* then, which apparently set out to underline the importance of sex, sexuality is seen to be meaningful only within a stable (and heterosexual) relationship. This diverges significantly from the emphasis given sex in the 1970s films when it was a matter of the individual's, rather than the couple's, interest.

The neo-traditional romantic comedy's insistence that sex does not matter runs against the significance accorded to sexual matters in the other sub-genres. In the screwball this was attained through *mise-en-scène* and suggestive dialogue and situation; in the sex comedy through the basic premises and racy innuendo; and in the radical romcom by clearly demonstrating the importance of sexual fulfilment to both sexes and the unwavering stare of the camera at embarrassed bodies experiencing desire and frustration. It seems significant that the strongest and most successful strand of counter-influence to the neo-traditional romantic comedy at present should be the very one most opposing its insistence on the relative unimportance of sex to romance. This contemporary cycle of *hommecoms*, which imports elements of the teen and gross-out movie, including their accent on physical urges and bodily emissions, seems currently to offer the best opportunity for a departure from the *sterility* affecting the dominant generic form.

As noted above, films like *Wedding Crashers* and *The 40 Year Old Virgin* can be posited as being, ultimately, as traditional as the usual female-centred comedies, when they abandon their insistence that sex is an important part of the individual's life and replace it with their final-reel emphasis on coupled sex. However, the films' opening scenarios and dominant sections of their narratives are devoted to emphasising the importance of sexual fulfilment. In this they can be seen to be the true heirs of the 1970s radical romantic comedy far more than those more conventional films which adopt the visual and aural textures of *Annie Hall* or *An Unmarried Woman*, only to ignore the ideologies that gave those textures their original significance. Although there seems to be a crisis of faith observable in the current stale products of the genre, it is to be hoped that the romantic comedy will continue to evolve, perhaps by overcoming its current aversion to sex and thus allowing future films to reflect the importance erotic attraction plays within human life, and has played in the greatest romantic comedies of former years.

NOTES

Introduction

1   This term is popularly used on both sides of the Atlantic as shorthand for romantic
    comedy, analogous with 'sitcom' as a truncation of 'situation comedy'; it is pej-
    orative to the extent that it implies adherence to a slick formula.

Chapter one

1   Consider, for example, this comment on *Failure to Launch* which *Sight and Sound*
    calls 'an uneasy collection of scenes which aren't quite slapstick and *non sequiturs*
    masquerading as one-liners, which are pegged onto an utterly formulaic rom-com
    plot' (Wood 2006: 50).
2   This trope has not died out: in *Serendipity* (2001) the characters played by John
    Cusack and Kate Beckinsale meet when both reach for the same pair of gloves in a
    department store sale; the symbolism of the pair each searching for the facsimile of
    a hand to hold is made much of in the film.
3   Amongst other very satisfying pieces, Ian Garwood (2000) focuses on the music of
    Sleepless in Seattle; Julia Lesage (1982) looks at the *mise-en-scène* of *An Unmarried
    Woman* and Madelyn Ritrosky-Winslow (2006) analyses intertextuality in the *Bridget
    Jones* films.
4   An indication: the catalogue of the British Film Institute Library, accessed 27 June
    2006, listed 398 books on the western, 340 on science fiction, 227 on the musical
    and 318 on film noir, in contrast to just 11 on the romantic comedy.
5   'While most romantic comedies are aimed at us girls, there are some that appeal

to the more testosterone-fuelled members of the audience...' (Berry & Errigo 2004: 38).

6   'Forget the football, watch the perfect match!'

Chapter two

1   For example, Robin Wood includes *Monkey Business* (1952) in his list of classic screwballs and also makes a case for *My Best Friend's Wedding* (1997) as belonging to the classic form (2001: 15).

Chapter three

1   1966 was a spy-mad year. Looking through *Variety* film reviews, from 1940 onwards, one hits an incredible slew of spy films where there were none or next to none before: 22 (out of 417 films); there are 12 in 1967, then back to average numbers in 1968 with 4. *Variety* itself commented on the trend in the review for *The Liquidator*: 'The flow of spy yarns, mainly spoofs in varying degrees, shows no sign of dwindling.'

Chapter five

1   We can compare such moments as when Reuben (Ben Stiller) suffers explosive diarrhoea at Polly's (Jennifer Aniston) apartment, and the confession from Sandy (Philip Seymour Hoffman) that he has 'sharted', with more conventional moments such as Reuben's reunion with Polly at the end.

2   Julia Lesage reads this scene in a different light: 'Visually what we see in these final shots is that the man has, even in his absence, taken over and even crippled the woman as an actor in public space' (1982: 88). While I take her point, I think it is complicated by the fact that Erica could abandon the painting at any time, and does not.

Conclusion

1   Peter Krämer notes assumed female genres comprise 'romantic comedy, musicals, melodrama/weepies, costume drama' (1999b: 94).

APPENDICES

Appendix A: key films synopses

My Man Godfrey (Gregory La Cava, 1936, US)
Irene Bullock (Carole Lombard), a spoiled rich girl, is on a scavenger hunt with her family, including sister Cornelia (Gail Patrick), mother (Alice Brady) and father (Eugene Palette). The hunt requires finding a variety of useless objects: as Irene explains, 'a scavenger hunt is exactly like a treasure hunt, except in a treasure hunt you try to find something you want and in a scavenger hunt you try to find something that *nobody* wants'. The final 'thing' needed to win Irene the competition is a 'forgotten man', a contemporary reference to the subject of President Roosevelt's 1932 speech about the typical law-abiding citizen of America who, as he causes no trouble, remains overlooked by politicians (also referenced in the grand musical finale of *Gold Diggers of 1933*. The team drives to the city dump and finds a forgotten man: this is Godfrey (William Powell), a dignified individual who takes a dislike to Cornelia, but agrees to accompany Irene so that she can beat her sister in the competition. With Godfrey inspected by the master of the hunt and pronounced authentic, Irene is declared the winner. Godfrey, pressed to make a speech, denounces the 'empty-headed nitwits' assembled before him, the film implying that they have lost their humanity in denying Godfrey his. The gathering is shocked at his bad manners: Irene, alone, is ashamed of her behaviour, and offers Godfrey the job of family butler. Ensconced in the Bullock mansion Godfrey soon succeeds in dealing so expertly with the foibles of the various family members that they all come to rely on him; and the maid, Cornelia and Irene become enamoured of his personal charms too.

Irene attempts to make Godfrey jealous by announcing her engagement to another man; Godfrey disappoints her by being pleased, however. Cornelia, less ditzy and more cruel than her sister, notices one guest's obvious recognition of Godfrey, and commits resources to finding out his true identity. This is eventually revealed: he is the son of a wealthy Boston family who abandoned his playboy lifestyle when jilted by a fiancée. Reassured of his entitlement to high status, Cornelia propositions Godfrey; when he rejects her, she hides a valuable bracelet in his bed so that he will be sent to jail. The police fail to find the incriminating item, however, and both Bullock girls are despatched to Europe by their enraged father. Returning months later they find the family fortunes have been depleted. Godfrey, however, has monitored the situation and steps in to save the family from ruin, having found and pawned the bracelet, investing the money for just such an occasion. He is greeted as the family hero, but characteristically denies this, excusing his gesture as self-interested: he has bought the city dump with investment profits, and turned it into an exclusive nightclub, thus giving all the other forgotten men steady employment. He thanks the Bullocks for the opportunities they gave him and leaves. Irene pursues him giddily, rushing to the nightclub, urging Godfrey to admit he cannot get rid of her, and bringing in a minister to marry them at once.

Pillow Talk (Michael Gordon, 1959, US)

Interior decorator Jan (Doris Day) and songwriter Brad (Rock Hudson) share a party line which he monopolises. The pair argue by phone but do not meet in person until Brad overhears a conversation in a nightclub and realises the very attractive woman being addressed is his line sharer, whom he had imagined an old maid. Realising she will never date him as himself, he spontaneously masquerades as 'Rex Stetson', a Texan oil millionaire, and begins to woo her. He also enjoys telephoning her, as himself, to warn that 'Rex' is probably either a wolf or, worse, does not like *women* at all, eventually making Jan anxious about whether 'Rex' desires her. 'Rex' tells Jan that he has to go away for the weekend and she invites herself along; the couple are about to consummate their relationship when Jan realises who Brad really is. Jan tells Brad she never wants to see him again, despite his protestations of love, and returns to the city. He hires her to redecorate his apartment, hoping that she will realise this is a marriage proposal, but she makes the place look like a brothel. Brad angrily bursts into her apartment and carries her across the city to his place, where he finally asks her to marry him.

Annie Hall (Woody Allen, 1977, US)
New Yorker Alvy Singer (Woody Allen) recounts the story of his break-up with girl-friend Annie Hall (Diane Keaton), prompting him to reminisce about his two failed marriages, his initial meeting with Annie, a disastrous trip to meet her family, his growing success as a stand-up comedian and her attempts to start a singing career. While Annie is neurotic and lacking in self-confidence, Alvy seems comfort-able with her, advising her on what books to read and films to see, sending her to a psychoanalyst so that she can begin to understand herself. When this improve-ment programme seems to be working, however, and Annie's career blossoms, leading to her greater independence from Alvy, he becomes needy and suspicious of her new friends. The couple split up and date others, then get back together for a time, but their differences of character and ambition cause too much friction. After a trip to Los Angeles which Manhattanite Alvy hates but Annie enjoys, the two split again. Alvy finds he cannot concentrate on work and feels miserable: he flies to LA to insist that Annie marry him but she refuses. Back in New York Alvy replays the scene of their meeting with different actors playing him and Annie, but this time she capitulates and there is a happy ending. Acknowledging the clichéd nature of this, Alvy shrugs and admits this scene was from his first stage play, not based on what really happened between himself and Annie. He finally relates that they met again in New York, Annie having moved back there, and went out for lunch and to talk about old times. As the film shows us scenes of their past romance, we hear Annie performing 'Seems Like Old Times', and, as the song ends on an empty street, with both former lovers having departed, the film ends too.

You've Got Mail (Nora Ephron, 1998, US)
Kathleen Kelly (Meg Ryan) and Joe Fox (Tom Hanks) are rival booksellers, she owning a children's bookstore she has inherited from her mother, he running an empire of discounted book warehouses. They are also secret email pen-pals, unwittingly corresponding under the aliases of 'NY152' and 'Shopgirl', and falling in love. Each has a steady partner too, but both Joe's girlfriend Patricia (Parker Posey) and Kathleen's boyfriend (Greg Kinnear) are shallow, selfish and career-mad. Kathleen and Joe both yearn for something more – something their mys-terious email pal supplies. Joe and Kathleen meet in real life when he visits her bookstore, and realises she is the one who his new superstore across the road will probably put out of business. They are attracted to each other, but Joe keeps his identity secret so that Kathleen does not throw him out of the store. Eventually they meet again at a party, and this time Kathleen is told who Joe is: they insult

each other. Sales at Kathleen's bookstore begin to suffer dramatically as her customers and authors desert her for the glamorous superstore. She enlists Frank to help mount a campaign to save the store, and ends up insulting Joe again, this time on television, much to his fury. At the same time, NY152 and Shopgirl have decided to meet at a coffee shop. When he gets there, Joe sees Kathleen and works out the truth, but decides not to tell her. The pair again talk and Kathleen insults him, but largely from misery at having been stood up.

NY152 apologises for not showing up and the pair go back to emailing regularly. Kathleen realises she will have to close the shop. Having done so, she succumbs to a cold and takes to her bed. Both Joe and Patricia and Frank and Kathleen break up. Joe feels bad about the shop's closure and goes to see Kathleen at her flat, asking if they can be friends. They begin to meet for coffee and walks around the city, and Kathleen tells him about her email admirer. He teases her relentlessly about him, urging her to meet NY152. When Kathleen realises the truth, she cries, and the couple kiss.

Appendix B: commonly employed romantic comedy tropes, with filmic examples

Trope	Films
Falling over, slapstick	*It Happened One Night; 20th Century; My Man Godfrey; Nothing Sacred; Bringing Up Baby; That Touch of Mink; Sleepless in Seattle; You've Got Mail; Two Weeks' Notice; Kate and Leopold; Hitch*
Adversarial relationship turning to love	*It Happened One Night; 20th Century; Bringing Up Baby; Pillow Talk; Lover Come Back; You've Got Mail; 10 Things I Hate About You; Animal Attraction; Two Weeks' Notice*
Break-up and makeup	*It Happened One Night; Pillow Talk; Lover Come Back; How to Lose a Guy in 10 Days; Something's Gotta Give; Hitch*
Her friend's advice vs. his friend's advice	*When Harry Met Sally; How to Lose a Guy in 10 Days; Hitch; A Lot Like Love*
Idiotic public gesture	*My Best Friend's Wedding; 10 Things I Hate About You; A Lot Like Love; Hitch*
Love montage	*Pillow Talk; Lover Come Back; How to Lose a Guy in 10 Days; Something's Gotta Give*
Masquerade	*My Man Godfrey; Pillow Talk; Lover Come Back; Only You; While You Were Sleeping; The Truth About Cats and Dogs; You've Got Mail; Three to Tango*

Trope	Films
Meet cute	*Bluebeard's Eight Wife; Bringing Up Baby; That Touch of Mink; Sleepless in Seattle; Serendipity; Maid in Manhattan; 50 First Dates*
Rules of romance	*Swingers; The Tao of Steve; Animal Attraction; The Sweetest Thing; 40 Days and 40 Nights; How to Lose a Guy in 10 Days; Hitch*
Wedding that goes wrong but it's just as well	*It Happened One Night; The Bride Came C.O.D; While You Were Sleeping; Runaway Bride; Sweet Home Alabama; Wedding Crashers*

FILMOGRAPHY

A Lot Like Love (Nigel Cole, 2005, US)
A Very Special Favour (Michael Gordon, 1965, US)
Alex and Emma (Rob Reiner, 2003, US)
Along Came Polly (John Hamburg, 2004, US)
American Pie (Paul Weitz, 1999, US)
An Affair to Remember (Leo McCarey, 1957, US)
Annie Hall (Woody Allen, 1977, US)
An Unmarried Woman (Paul Mazursky, 1978, US)
Animal Attraction (Tony Goldwyn, 2001, US)
Annie Hall (Woody Allen, 1977, US)
The Apartment (Billy Wilder, 1960, US)
The Awful Truth (Leo McCarey, 1937, US)
Babes on Broadway (Busby Berkeley, 1941, US)
The Band Wagon (Vincente Minnelli, 1953, US)
Bluebeard's Eighth Wife (Ernst Lubitsch, 1938, US)
Bob & Carol & Ted & Alice (Paul Mazursky, 1969, US)
Breakfast at Tiffany's (Blake Edwards, 1961, US)
The Bride Came C.O.D. (William Keighley, 1941, US)
Bridget Jones's Diary (Sharon Maguire, 2001, UK)
Bridget Jones: The Edge of Reason (Beeban Kidron, 2004, UK)
Bring It On (Peyton Reed, 2000, US)
Bringing Down the House (Adam Shankman, 2003, US)
Bringing Up Baby (Howard Hawks, 1938, US)
Brown Sugar (Rick Famuyiwa, 2002, US)
Casablanca (Michael Curtiz, 1942, US)
Clueless (Amy Heckerling, 1995, US)
Come Blow Your Horn (Bud Yorkin, 1963, US)
Come September (Robert Mulligan, 1961, US)
Date Movie (Aaron Seltzer, 2006, US)
The Daytrippers (Greg Mottola, 1996, US)

Denise Calls Up (Hal Salwen, 1995, US)

The Dirty Dozen (Robert Aldrich, 1967, US)

Doctor, You've Got to be Kidding! (Peter Tewkesbury, 1966, US)

Down With Love (Peyton Reed, 2004, US)

Emma (Douglas McGrath, 1996, US/UK)

Failure to Launch (Tom Dey, 2006, US)

50 First Dates (Peter Segal, 2004, US)

40 Days and 40 Nights (Michael Lehmann, 2002, US)

The 40 Year Old Virgin (Judd Apatow, 2005, US)

48 Hrs (Walter Hill, 1982, US)

Four Weddings and a Funeral (Mike Newell, 1994, UK)

Get Over It (Tommy O'Haver, 2001, US)

Go Fish (Rose Troche, 1994, US)

The Godfather (Francis Ford Coppola, 1972, US)

The Gold Diggers of 1933 (Mervyn LeRoy, 1933, US)

Gone With the Wind (Victor Fleming, 1939, US)

The Goodbye Girl (Herbert Ross, 1977, US)

The Graduate (Mike Nichols, 1967, US)

Green Card (Peter Weir, 1990, US)

Harold and Maude (Hal Ashby, 1971, US)

The Heartbreak Kid (Elaine May, 1972, US)

Hitch (Andy Tennant, 2005, US)

How to Lose a Guy in 10 Days (Donald Petrie, 2003, US)

How to Murder Your Wife (Richard Quine, 1965, US)

Imagine Me and You (Ol Parker, 2005, USA/UK/Germany)

It Happened One Night (Frank Capra, 1934, US)

Jeffrey (Christopher Ashley, 1995, US)

Jerry Maguire (Cameron Crowe, 1996, US)

Just Like Heaven (Mark Waters, 2005, US)

Kate and Leopold (James Mangold, 2003, US)

Kissing Jessica Stein (Charles Herman-Wermfeld, 2001, US)

L'Eclisse (*The Eclipse*) (Michelangelo Antonioni, 1962, France/Italy)

LA Story (Mick Jackson, 1991, US)

Laws of Attraction (Peter Howitt, 2004, US)

Les Quatre Cents Coups (*The 400 Blows*) (François Truffaut, 1959, France)

Lethal Weapon series (Richard Donner, 1987–98, US)

The Liquidator (Jack Cardiff, 1965, UK)

Losin' It (Curtis Hanson, 1983, US)

Love Story (Arthur Hiller, 1970, US)

Lover Come Back (Delbert Mann, 1961, US)

Maid in Manhattan (Wayne Wang, 2002, US)

Manhattan (Woody Allen, 1979, US)

Me, Myself and Irene (Farrelly Brothers, 2000, US)

Mean Streets (Martin Scorsese, 1973, US)

Monkey Business (Howard Hawks, 1952, US)

Monster in Law (Robert Luketic, 2005, US)

The Moon is Blue (Otto Preminger, 1953, US)

Moonstruck (Norman Jewison, 1987, US)

Move Over Darling (Michael Gordon, 1963, US)

Mr Blanding Builds His Dream House (H. C. Potter, 1948, US)

My Best Friend's Wedding (P. J. Hogan, 1997, US)

My Big Fat Greek Wedding (Joel Zwick, 2002, US)

My Favourite Wife (Garson Kanin, 1940, US)

My Man Godfrey (Gregory LaCava, 1936, US)

My Super Ex-Girlfriend (Ivan Reitman, 2006, US)

The Next Best Thing (John Schlesinger, 2000, US)

North By Northwest (Alfred Hitchcock, 1959, US)

Notting Hill (Roger Mitchell, UK, 1999, US)

The Object of My Affection (Nicholas Hytner, 1998, US)

On a Clear Day You Can See Forever (Vincente Minnelli, 1970, US)

Once Upon a Honeymoon (Leo McCarey, 1942, US)

Only You (Norman Jewison, 1994, US)

Our Man Flint (Daniel Mann, 1966, US)

The Out of Towners (Arthur Hiller, 1970, US)

The Parallax View (Alan J Pakula, 1974, US)

Phfft (Mark Robson, 1954, US)

Pillow Talk (Michael Gordon, 1959, US)

Porky's (Bob Clark, 1982, US)

Pretty Woman (Garry Marshall, 1990, US)

Prime (Ben Younger, 2006, US)

The Prince and Me (Martha Coolidge, 2004, US)

Roxanne (Fred Schepisi, 1987, US)

Runaway Bride (Garry Marshall, 1999, US)

Saving Face (Alice Wu, 2004, US)

Semi-Tough (Michael Ritchie, 1977, US)

Serendipity (Peter Chelsom, 2001, US)

Sex and the Single Girl (Richard Quine, 1964, US)

Shaft (Gordon Parks, 1971, US)

The Shop Around the Corner (Ernst Lubitsch, 1940, US)

The Silencers (Phil Karlson, 1966, US)

Sleepless in Seattle (Nora Ephron, 1993, US)

Snow White and the Seven Dwarfs (Ben Sharpsteen, 1939, US)

Some Like It Hot (Billy Wilder, 1959, US)

Something's Gotta Give (Nancy Meyer, 2003, US)

The Sorrow and the Pity (*Le Chagrin et la pitié*) (Marcel Ophuls, 1969, France/
    Switzerland/West Germany)

South Pacific (Joshua Logan, 1958, US)

Starting Over (Alan J. Pakula, 1979, US)

Sunday in New York (Peter Tewkesbury, 1963, US)

Superfly (Gordon Parks Jnr, 1972, US)

Sweet Home Alabama (Andy Tennant, 2002, US)

The Sweetest Thing (Roger Kumble, 2002, US)

Swingers (Doug Liman, 1996, US)

The Tao of Steve (Jenniphr Goodman, 2000, US)

Taxi Driver (Martin Scorsese, 1976, US)

10 (Blake Edwards, 1979, US)

10 Things I Hate About You (Gil Junger, 1999, US)

The Tender Trap (Charles Walters, 1955, US)

That Touch of Mink (Delbert Mann, 1962, US)

There's Something About Mary (Farrelly Brothers, 1998, US)

Three Days of the Condor (Stanley Pollack, 1975, US)

Three to Tango (Damon Santostefano, 1999, US)

The Thrill of it All (Norman Jewison, 1963, US)

To Be or Not to Be (Ernst Lubitsch,1942, US)

Tootsie (Sydney Pollack, 1982, US)

Top Gun (Tony Scott, 1986, US)

Touch of Pink (Ian Iqbal Rasid, 2004, Canada/UK)

The Truth About Cats and Dogs (Michael Lehmann, 1996, US)

20th Century (Howard Hawks, 1934, US)

Two Tickets to Broadway (James V Kern, 1951, US)

Two Weeks' Notice (Marc Lawrence, 2002, US)

Under the Yum Yum Tree (David Swift, 1963, US)
Up the Sandbox (Irvin Kershner, 1972, US)
Wedding Crashers (David Dobkin, 2005, US)
The Wedding Date (Clare Kilner, 2005, US)
The Wedding Planner (Adam Shankman, 2001, US)
The Wedding Singer (Frank Coraci, 1998, US)
What Women Want (Nancy Meyers, 2000, US)
What's Up, Doc? (Peter Bogdanovich, 1972, US)
When Harry Met Sally (Rob Reiner, 1989, US)
Where Were You When the Lights Went Out? (Hy Averback, 1968, US)
While You Were Sleeping (Jon Turteltaub, 1995, US)
Wimbledon (Richard Loncraine, 2004, UK)
The Wizard of Oz (Victor Fleming, 1939, US)
You've Got Mail (Nora Ephron, 1998, US)

BIBLIOGRAPHY

Altman, Rick (1998) 'Reusable Packaging: Generic Products and the Recycling Process', in Nick Browne (ed.) *Refiguring American Film Genres: History and Theory*. Berkeley: University of California Press.

Anon. (1953) Editorial, *Playboy*, November/December, 1, 1.

___ (1971) Review of *Harold and Maude*, *Variety Film Reviews*, vol. 13. New York: Garland.

___ (1972) Review of *Up the Sandbox*, *Variety Film Reviews*, vol. 13. New York: Garland.

Babington, Bruce and Peter William Evans (1989) *Affairs to Remember: The Hollywood Comedy of the Sexes*. Manchester: Manchester University Press.

Berry, Jo and Angie Errigo (2004) *Chick Flicks: Movies Women Love*. London: Orion Books.

Betts, Hannah (2005) 'Now you can try dating, Austen-Style', *Times*, 27 August,; http://entertainment.timesonline.co.uk/article/0,,14931-1751929,00.html (accessed 21 November).

'Bige' (1936) Review of *My Man Godfrey*, *Variety Film Reviews*, vol. 5. New York: Garland.

Bonila, Paul C. (2005) 'Is there more to Hollywood Lowbrow than meets the eye?', *Quarterly Review of Film and Video*, 22, 17–24.

Borde, Raymond and Etienne Chaumeton (2002 [1955]) *A Panorama of American Film Noir 1941–1953*, trans. Paul Hammond. San Francisco: City Lights Books.

Bordwell, David (1979) 'The art cinema as a mode of filmmaking', *Film Criticism*, 4, 56–64.

Bordwell, David and Kristin Thompson (2003) *Film Art: An Introduction*, seventh edition, New York: McGraw Hill.

Britton, Andrew (1986) 'Cary Grant: Comedy and male desire', *CineAction*, 7,

37–51.

Byrge, Duane and Robert Milton Miller (1991) *The Screwball Comedy Films: A History and Filmography 1934–1942*. Jefferson, NC: McFarland.

Carson, Diane (1994) 'To be seen but not heard: *The Awful Truth*', in Diane Carson, Linda Dittmar and Janice Welsch (eds) *Multiple Voices in Feminist Film Criticism*. Minneapolis: University of Minnesota Press, 213–25.

Cavell, Stanley (1981) *Pursuits of Happiness: The Hollywood Comedy of Remarriage*. Cambridge, MA: Harvard University Press.

Chandler, Charlotte (2002) *Nobody's Perfect: Billy Wilder, A Personal Biography*. New York: Simon and Schuster.

'Chic' (1934) Review of *It Happened One Night*, *Variety Film Reviews*, vol. 5. New York: Garland.

Cochrane, Kira (2006) 'Thongs, implants and the death of real passion', *Guardian*, 21 June, 6–9.

Doane, Mary Anne (1987) *The Desire to Desire: The Women's Film of the 1940s*. Bloomington: Indiana University Press.

Dowdy, Andrew (1973) *The Films of the Fifties: The American State of Mind*. New York: William Morrow.

Dreisinger, Baz (2000) 'The queen in shining armour: safe eroticism and the gay friend', *Journal of Popular Film and Television*, 28, 1, 2–11.

Everson, William K. (1994) *Hollywood Bedlam: Classic Screwball Comedies*. New York: Citadel Press.

Felperin, Leslie (2005) Review of *Imagine Me and You*, *Variety*, 24–30 October, 26.

Fuchs, Cynthia (1997) 'Framing and passing in *Pillow Talk*', in Joel Foreman (ed.) *The Other Fifties: Interrogating Midcentury American Icons*. Urbana and Chicago: University of Illinois Press, 224–51.

Garwood, Ian (2000) 'Must you remember this? Orchestrating the "standard" pop song in *Sleepless in Seattle*', *Screen*, 41, 3, 282–98.

Gehring, Wes (ed.) (1988) *Handbook of American Film Genres*. New York: Greenwood Press.

____ (2002) *Romantic vs. Screwball Comedy: Charting the Difference*. Maryland: Scarecrow Press, Inc.

Gollin, Richard M. (1992) *A Viewer's Guide to Film: Arts, Artifices, and Issues*. New York: McGraw Hill.

Grant, Barry Keith (2007) *Film Genre: From Iconography to Ideology*. London: Wallflower Press.

Hampton, Howard (2004) 'True romance: on the current state of date movies', *Film Comment*, November/December, 30–4.

Harvey, James (1998) *Romantic Comedy in Hollywood, From Lubitsch to Sturges*.

New York: Da Capo Press.

Haskell, Molly (1974) *From Reverence to Rape: The Treatment of Women in the Movies*. New York: Penguin.

Henderson, Brian (1978) 'Romantic comedy today: semi-tough or impossible?', *Film Quarterly*, 31, 4, 11–23.

Henderson, Lauren (2005) *Jane Austen's Guide to Dating*. London: Hodder Headline.

Kendall, Elizabeth (1990) *The Runaway Bride: Hollywood Romantic Comedy of the 1930s*. New York: Alfred R. Knopf.

King, Geoff (2002) *Film Comedy*. London: Wallflower Press.

Kinsey, Alfred C., Wardell B. Pomeroy, Clyde E. Martin and Paul H. Gebhard (1953) *Sexual Behaviour in the Human Female*. Philadelphia and London: W. B. Saunders Company.

Koehler, Robert (2003) Review of *How to Lose a Guy in 10 Days*, *Variety*, 3–9 February, 68–9.

Krämer, Peter (1999a) 'Women first: *Titanic*, action-adventure films, and Hollywood's female audience', in Kevin Sandler and Gaylyn Studlar (eds) *Titanic: Anatomy of a Blockbuster*. New Brunswick, NJ: Rutgers University Press, 108–31.

____ (1999b) 'A powerful cinema-going force? Hollywood and female audiences since the 1960s', in Melvyn Stokes and Richard Maltby (eds) *Identifying Hollywood's Audiences: Cultural Identity and the Movies*. London: British Film Institute, 93–108.

Krutnik, Frank (1990) 'The faint aroma of performing seals: The "nervous" romance and the comedy of the sexes', *Velvet Light Trap*, 26, 57–72.

____ (1998) 'Love lies: Romantic fabrication in contemporary romantic comedy', in Peter William Evans and Celestino Deleyto (eds) (1998) *Terms of Endearment: Hollywood Romantic Comedy of the 1980s and 1990s*. Edinburgh: Edinburgh University Press, 15–36.

Leff, Leonard J. and Jerold L. Simmonds (2001) *The Dame in the Kimono: Hollywood, Censorship and the Production Code*, revised edition. Lexington: University Press of Kentucky.

Lesage, Julia (1982) 'The hegemonic female fantasy in *An Unmarried Woman* and *Craig's Wife*', *Film Reader*, 5, 83–94.

Levy, Ariel (2005) *Female Chauvinist Pigs: Women and the Rise of Raunch Culture*. New York: Simon and Schuster.

'Mack' (1977) Review of *Annie Hall*, *Variety Film Reviews*, vol. 14. New York: Garland.

Matheou, Demetrios (2003) Review of *Hope Springs*, *Sight and Sound*, May, 48.

McArthur, Colin (1972) *Underworld USA*. London: Secker & Warburg.

McCallum, E. L. (1999) 'Mother talk: Maternal masquerade and the problem of the single girl', *Camera Obscura*, 42, 71–94.

Modleski, Tania (1984) 'Time and desire in the women's film', *Cinema Journal* 23, 3, 19–30.

Mulvey, Laura (1986) 'Melodrama in and out of the home', in Colin McCabe (ed.) *High Theory/Low Culture: Analyzing Popular Television and Film*. Manchester: Manchester University Press, 80–100.

'Murf' (1972) Review of *What's Up, Doc?*, *Variety Film Reviews*, vol. 13. New York: Garland.

Musser, Charles (1995) "Divorce, DeMille and the comedy of remarriage" in Kristine Brunovska Karnick and Henry Jenkins (eds), *Classical Hollywood Comedy*. New York: Routledge, 282–313.

Neale, Steve (1992) 'The big romance or something wild?: Romantic comedy today', *Screen*, 33, 3, 284–99.

_____ (2000) *Genre and Hollywood*. London: Routledge.

_____ (ed.) (2002) *Genre and Contemporary Hollywood*. London: British Film Institute.

Negra, Diane (2006) 'Where the boys are: Postfeminism and the new single man', *Flow*, 4, 3; http://jot.communication.utexas.edu/flow/?jot=view&id=1724 (accessed 14 June).

Nochimson, Martha P. (2002) *Screen Couple Chemistry: The Power of 2*. Austin: University of Texas Press.

Paul, William (2002) 'The impossibility of romance: Hollywood comedy, 1978–1999' in Steve Neale (ed.) *Genre and Contemporary Hollywood*. London: British Film Institute, 117–29.

Quart, Leonard and Albert Auster (1991) *American Film and Society Since 1945*. New York: Praeger. 2nd edition.

Rickman, Gregg (ed.) (2001) *Film Comedy Reader*. New York: Limelight Editions.

Ritrosky-Winslow, Madelyn (2006) 'Colin & Renée & Mark & Bridget: The intertextual crowd', *Quarterly Review of Film and Video*, 23, 237–56.

Rowe, Kathleen (1995) *The Unruly Woman: Gender and the Genres of Laughter*. Austin: University of Texas Press.

Rubinfeld, Mark D. (2001) *Bound to Bond: Gender, Genre and the Hollywood Romantic Comedy*. New York: Praeger.

Schatz, Thomas (1981) *Hollywood Genres: Formulas, Filmmaking and the Studio System*. New York: McGraw Hill, Inc.

Sennett, Ted (1973) *Lunatics and Lovers: A Tribute to the Giddy and Glittering Era of the Screen's 'Screwball' and Romantic Comedies*. New Rochelle, NY: Arlington House.

Shary, Timothy (2002) *Generation Multiplex: The Image of Youth in Contemporary*

American Cinema. Austin: University of Texas Press.

____ (2005) *Teen Movies: American Youth on Screen.* London: Wallflower Press.

Shumway, David R. (2003) *Modern Love: Romance, Intimacy and the Marriage Crisis.* New York and London: New York University Press.

Sikov, Ed (1989) *Screwball: Hollywood's Madcap Romantic Comedies.* New York: Crown.

____ (1998) *On Sunset Boulevard: The Life and Times of Billy Wilder.* New York: Hyperion Books.

Vineberg, Steve (2005) *High Comedy in American Movies. Class and Humour From the 1920s to the Present.* Lanham, Maryland: Rowman and Littlefield Publishers, Inc.

Walker, Alexander (1966) 'The Last American Massacre: Rock Hudson & Co.', in *The Celluloid Sacrifice: Aspects of Sex in the Movies.* London: Michael Joseph, 214–32.

Williams, Doug (2001) 'Introspective laughter: Nora Ephron and the American comedy Renaissance', in Gregg Rickman (ed.) *Film Comedy Reader.* New York: Limelight Editions, 341–62.

Wolfe, Tom (1976) *Mauve Gloves and Madmen, Clutter and Vine.* New York: Farrar, Strauss and Giroux.

Wood, Robin (1976) 'Democracy and shpontanuity: Leo McCarey and the Hollywood tradition', *Film Comment*, Jan/Feb, 6–15.

____ (2001) 'Screwball and the masquerade: *The Lady Eve* and *Two-Faced Woman*', *CineAction*, 54, 12–19.

Wood, Anna (2003) Review of *How to Lose a Guy in 10 Days, Sight and Sound*, May, 50.

____ (2006) Review of *Failure to Launch, Sight and Sound*, June, 50.

INDEX